T
phrasebook

lonely planet

Tom Brosnahan

Turkish Phrasebook
 1st edition

Published by
 Lonely Planet Publications
 Head Office: PO Box 617, Hawthorn, Vic 3122, Australia
 US Office: PO Box 2001A, Berkeley, CA 94702, USA

Printed by
 Colorcraft Ltd, Hong Kong

Published
 April 1990

Editor	Chris Taylor
Design & cover design	Margaret Jung
Illustrations	Peter Flavelle, Graham Imeson, Ann Jeffree & Valerie Tellini

National Library of Australia Cataloguing in Publication Data

Brosnahan, Tom.
 Turkish Phrasebook.

 ISBN 0 86442 069 2.

 1. Turkish language – Conversation and phrase books – English. I. Title.
 1. Title.

494.3583421
© Copyright Lonely Planet 1990

Contents

Introduction

Turkish is so different from European languages that it can be bewildering at first. But it has advantages. There are no articles (a, an, the), no gender distinctions (he, she, it), only one irregular noun (*su* – water) and one irregular verb (*olmak* – to be). It also has a logical – if complex – structure. Context counts for a lot in Turkish, so you can say a few words and phrases to Turks and they will pick up the rest easily.

The Turkish language is a member of the Ural-Altaic language family, which also includes such lesser-known tongues as Kirghiz, Kazakh, Azerbaijani, Manchu, Chuvash, and Mongolian. Surprisingly, Korean is also a Ural-Altaic language.

'Pure' Oğuz Turkish, as spoken by nomads of Central Asia 1500 years ago, was a simple, logical and expressive language. When the Turks encountered Islam in AD 670, they adopted the Arabic alphabet, even though it was ill-suited to recording the sounds of Turkish.

As the erstwhile tribesmen gained worldliness and sophistication, their language took on grammatical and vocabulary borrowings from the Persians and the Arabs. At the height of the Ottoman Empire's power, the Turkish spoken by the Ottoman upper classes was overly complex, full of flowery phrases and wordy academic usages.

After the fall of the empire, Kemal Atatürk undertook to reform and 'purify' Turkish to encourage literacy. He established the Turkish Language Society, with instructions for it to rid the Turkish language of Arabic and Persian words and grammatical usages, and to replace them with revitalised Turkish ones. Thus, one could now say 'you', instead of 'your exalted personage' (Persian), and 'me', instead of 'your humble servant.'

Also in the interests of literacy, Atatürk ordered that the Arabic alphabet be abandoned in favour of a modified Latin one. On 1 November 1928, Parliament decreed that after two months no published materials could be in Arabic script, but only in the modern Turkish alphabet. Atatürk himself took blackboard and chalk to village squares and taught the new letters to the people. In ensuing years, Turkish changed so drastically that today's Turkish school child or university student cannot read Ottoman works of a century ago without special instruction in alphabet, grammar and vocabulary. Indeed, Turkish has changed so much since the 1930s that even Atatürk's speeches (he died in 1938) seem archaic and mysterious today. Most have been 'translated' into *öztürkçe*, the modern 'pure Turkish'.

The language reforms introduced many new or 'revived' words and phrases into Turkish. Thus you may find that there are two or more ways to say something: the 'old' way and the 'new' way. Both ways are completely acceptable.

Modern Turkish is spoken by the nearly 60 million citizens of the Turkish Republic and also by Turkish Cypriots and small communities of ethnic Turks in Greece. Ethnic Turkish minorities in Bulgaria and Yugoslavia speak dialects of Ottoman Turkish. If you can speak

Turkish, you can make yourself understood from Belgrade, Yugoslavia, to Xinjiang, China.

At the suggestion of readers of my guidebook, *Turkey – a travel survival kit,* I've made up a cassette tape to help you learn correct Turkish pronunciation and useful phrases. Pronunciation is important; a word mispronounced may have a different meaning altogether. For your copy of the cassette, send a cheque payable to Tom Brosnahan for US$10, A$12.50, UK£6, CN$12, or SFr16 to Turkish Cassette, c/o Tom Brosnahan, PO Box 563, Concord, MA 01742, USA.

Pronunciation

Despite daunting oddities such as the 'soft g' (ğ) and the 'undotted i' (ı), Turkish is phonetic and fairly easy to pronounce. Note that each Turkish letter is pronounced; there are no diphthongs (double-letter sounds like 'th' or 'ch') as in English, and there is only one silent (unpronounced) letter, the ğ.

Vowels

A, a	as the 'a' in 'art' or 'bar'
E, e	as the 'e' in 'ever' or 'fell'
İ, i	as the 'ee' in 'see'
I, ı	as the vowel sound in 'were' or 'sir'
O, o	as the 'o' in 'hot'
Ö, ö	as the 'ur' in 'fur'
U, u	as the 'oo' in 'moo' or the 'oe' in 'shoe'
Ü, ü	as a German or French 'u'; similar to the the 'ew' in 'few'

Turkish has two very different sounds represented by the letter 'i'. To differentiate them, one 'i' has a dot, the other one has no dot. It's easy for your eye to ignore this difference when you read, so you must stay alert. Note that *ısırır* is pronounced 'UH-suh-RUHR', but that *ikinci* is pronounced 'ee-KEEN-jee'. Keep your eye out for the dot on the capital *I* as well: *Isparta* is pronounced 'uhss-SPAHR-tah' not 'eess-SPAHR-tah', and *İzmir* is pronounced 'EEZ-meer'.

As for *ö* and *ü*, purse your lips when saying them. For *ü*, shape your lips to say 'oo', but then say 'ee'.

8

Vowel Harmony

Turkish divides vowels into two groups: those formed 'in the front of the mouth' (*e, i, ö, ü*) and those formed 'in the back of the mouth' (*a, ı, o, u*). This odd distinction is very important when forming words with suffixes because the vowel(s) in the suffix(es) must be of the same type as the vowel(s) in the root word. For example, *hepinizi*, 'all of you', is formed by taking the root *hep*, 'all', and adding the suffix *-iniz*, 'you' and the suffix *-i*, 'of'. The *e* of *hep* and the *i*'s of *-inizi* have vowel harmony because both are 'front' vowels. You can't use the forms of the suffix made with an undotted i (*-ınızı*) because *ı* is a 'back' vowel. To form *arabanızı*, 'your car', from *araba*, 'car', and *- ınızı*, 'you', using *ı* would be correct because the vowels in *araba* are all 'back' vowels and so is *ı*.

After a while you'll get a feel for vowel harmony and won't have to think about it. And even if you make mistakes, you will probably still be understood.

Consonants

Most consonants are pronounced as in English. Of the exceptions, the most unusual and bothersome is *c*, which is always pronounced like an English 'j', but which you will frustratingly pronounce as 'k' for the first few days in Turkey.

C, c	as the 'j' in 'jet' or 'jigsaw'
Ç, ç	as the 'ch' in 'church'
G, g	always hard; as the 'g' in 'get', not as in 'gentle'
ǧ	silent; lengthens preceding vowel (see overleaf)
H, h	unvoiced; as the 'h' in 'half'
J, j	as the 'z' in 'azure'
S, s	unvoiced; as the 's' in 'stress', not as the 's' in 'ease'

Ş, ş   as the 'sh' in 'show'
V, v   as the 'w' in 'weather'

The 'soft g' (ğ) is never pronounced, and it never begins a word. It lengthens the preceding vowel slightly, but you can ignore it altogether. Whatever you do, don't pronounce it. Examples: *tuğra* is 'TOO-rah', not 'tura'; *soğan* sounds like English 'so on' not 'sewn'.

The Turkish *h*, however, is pronounced, though always unvoiced (aspirated). Start saying 'hot', but stop with the 'h'. That's the sound. It never combines with any other letter to form one sound. Thus *mithat* is pronounced 'meet-HOT', not like the English word 'methought', and *meshut* is 'mess- HOOT', not 'meh-SHOOT'.

The Turkish *v* is soft – halfway between an English 'v' and 'w'. When a Turk says 'very,' it sounds to us like 'wery'.

Double Consonants

Double consonants like *kk* in *dikkat* or *bb* in *tıbbi* are held longer. For instance, *tıbbi* sounds like 'tub bee', not like 'to be'. You'll have no trouble with double consonants if you imagine that the first consonant is ending a word and the second is beginning a new word. Thus, *yollar* is pronounced 'yol lar', not 'yolar'.

Grammar

Turkish is a systematic and logical language with no gender distinction, only one irregular noun (*su* – water) and one irregular verb (*olmak* – to be). It is an agglutinative language: suffixes are added to a short word-root to form an adjective, noun, verb, or verbal noun. If several suffixes are added, a single word can become an entire sentence. This method of using 'building blocks' to make words is sensible, but so different from what English speakers are used to that it can be very confusing at first. Still, if you learn to use several important suffixes, you'll be able to express yourself.

The grammar rules for use of suffixes are logical, but the rules are complicated somewhat by the need for certain 'buffer' letters *s*, *n*, or *y*, added for ease of pronunciation with certain combinations of words and suffixes. You will probably still be understood most of the time, even if you ignore these rules or make mistakes.

Word Order

Pronouns, nouns and adjectives usually come first, then the verb. The final suffix on the verb is the subject of the sentence:

I'll go to Istanbul.	*İstanbul'a gideceğim.*
	'Istanbul-to go-will-I'.
I want to buy (some) biscuits.	*Biskuvi almak istiyorum.*
	'Biscuits to-buy am wanting-I'.
We stayed for only one night.	*Yalnız bir gece kaldık.*
	'Only one night stayed-we'.

11

Some complex sentences can be merely a few long words packed
with suffixes:

Will those of the Americans supposedly be made more expensive?
   Amerikalılarının pahalılatılacaklar mıymış?

Noun Suffixes

A suffix may take one of several forms, depending upon vowel
harmony (see the Pronunciation chapter). For instance, the plural
suffix is *-ler* for root words with front vowels, and *-lar* for root
words with back vowels. Similarly, the suffix indicating 'to' is *-e*
for front vowels and *-a* for back vowels. I've given two examples
of each suffix below. The first example in each case uses front
vowels, the second one back vowels.

plural	*-ler, -lar*
meal – *yemek*	meals – *yemekler*
airplane – *uçak*	airplanes – *uçaklar*
to	*-e, -a*
sea – *deniz*	to the sea – *denize*
ship – *vapur*	to the ship – *vapura*
from	*-den, -dan*
hotel – *otel*	from the hotel – *otelden*
car – *araba*	from the car – *arabadan*
with, of, or characterised by	*-li, -lı, -lü, -lu*
meat – *et*	(a dish made) with meat – *etli*

shower – *duş* room – *oda*	room with shower – *duşlu oda*
yoghurt – *yoğurt*	kebap with yoghurt – *yoğurtlu kebap*
Ireland – *İrlonda*	Irish – *İrlondalı*

without	*-siz, -sız,-süz, -suz*
fee – *ücret*	without fee – *ücretsiz*
mind – *akıl*	mindless, stupid – *akılsız*

'-ness': makes a noun abstract	*-lik, -luk*
good – *iyi*	goodness – *iyilik*
traveller – *yolcu*	journey – *yolculuk*

'er': indicates a person who does/uses/makes/sells etc (something)	*-ci, -cı, -cü, -cu*
watch or clock – *saat*	watchmaker; watch or clock seller – *saatçi*
tea – *çay*	tea maker; teahouse waiter – *çaycı,*

Suffix Examples

Here are some examples of how suffixes can change the meaning of a root word:

key	*anahtar*
keys	*anahtarlar*
my key	*anahtarım*
your keys	*anahtarlarınız*
(the) key's ...	*anahtarın*

characterised by a key, having a key	*anahtarlı*
keyless	*anahtarsız*
'key thing' (key ring, key holder, etc)	*anahtarlık*
key-person (key cutter, locksmith)	*anahtarcı*

Possessive Pronouns

There are several ways to show possession. While not strictly correct, the easiest way is simply to use the possessive pronoun:

my/mine – *benim*	our/ours – *bizim*
your/yours – *senin*	your/yours (plural) – *sizin*
his/her/its – *onun*	their/theirs – *onların*

Here are some examples:

pen – *kalem*	your pen – *sizin kalem*
ticket – *bilet*	his ticket – *onun bilet*

Possessive Suffix

You can also add a suffix to a noun to show possession. This is fully correct:

my – *(i)m*	our – *(i)miz*
your – *(i)n*	your – *(i)niz*
his/her/its – *(s)i*	their – *leri*

Possessive suffixes, like others, are subject to vowel harmony, so it might be, for example, -*im* for one word, -*um* for another.

ticket – *bilet*	your ticket – *biletiniz*
suitcase – *bavul*	my suitcase – *bavulum*

Using either the possessive pronoun or the possessive suffix will allow you to make yourself understood. However, to emphasise ownership (as in 'not my pen, *your* pen'), use both the pronoun and the suffix together:

your – *sizin*	pen – *kalem*	your pen – *sizin kaleminiz*
his – *onun*	suitcase – *bavul*	his suitcase – *onun bavulu*

Adjectives

Turkish adjectives are simple and useful. Often an adjective and a noun have the same meaning. The adjective *genç*, for example, means 'young', but can also be used as a noun, 'a youth'.

Comparison

Comparison is easy in Turkish. Taking 'long', *uzun*, as an example, the comparative is formed by putting *daha* in front of it: *daha uzun* – 'longer'. For 'longest', put *en* in front of it: *en uzun*.

cheap	cheaper	cheapest
ucuz	*daha ucuz*	*en ucuz*
beautiful	more beautiful	most beautiful
güzel	*daha güzel*	*en güzel*
much, a lot	more	most
çok	*daha çok*	*en çok*

Verbs

Verb Suffixes

Turkish verbs also use suffixes to change the meaning of a simple root. This can be as simple as the combination of *gel-*, the root for 'come', and *-ir*, the suffix for the simple present tense, making *gelir*, 'he comes'. Or it can be as complicated as *gelmeyecek miymiştiniz?*, 'was it not reported that you would not have come?'

Tense

simple present	*-ar, -er, -ır, -ir, -ur, -ür*
he/she/it comes – *gelir*	
future	*-acak, -ecek, -acağ-, -eceğ-*
he/she/it will come – *gelecek*	
simple past	*-dı, -di, -du, -dü*
he/she/it came, arrived – *geldi*	
continuous (like '-ing')	*-ıyor, -iyor*
he/she/it is coming – *geliyor*	
infinitive ending	*-mak, -mek*
to come – *gelmek*	

The 3rd person singular (he/she/it) is the simplest form of the verb. To make the other forms, you must add other suffixes:

person	singular	plural
1st	I – *im*	we – *iz*
2nd	you – *sin*	you* – *siniz*
3rd	he/she/it – (no suffix)	they – *ler*

Here are some examples:

1st	I come – *gelirim*	we come – *geliriz*
2nd	you come – *gelirsin*	you come* – *gelirsiniz*
3rd	he/she/it comes – *gelir*	they come – *gelirler*

*Note that the 2nd person plural is also the formal singular. You can say *gelirsin* to a friend or relative, but to be polite you must say *gelirsiniz* to a stranger or important person. As a traveller it is best to always use the 2nd person plural form *-siniz*, whether talking to one Turk or several.

The preceding tense suffixes that apply to the verb *gel-* can change slightly according to the root of the verb, but the various forms of the suffix are all pretty similar. For instance, instead of *-ir* in *gelir* it might be *-ür* in *götürür*. But the tense suffix's main 'clue', the *r*, is always there.

The personal suffix also changes, according to vowel harmony, so it's *gelirim*, but *götürürüm*. In this case the personal suffix's main 'clue', the 'm', is always there.

Personal Pronouns with Verbs

I – *ben*   we – *biz*
you – *sen*   you – *siz*
he/she/it – *o*   they – *onlar*

Because the suffixes *-im*, *-iz*, *-sin*, *-siniz*, and *-ler* already tell you who is acting, personal pronouns are not really necessary. Turks use them mostly for emphasis or to make a point more clearly. In other words, *gelirim* and *ben gelirim* mean the same thing: 'I come'. Here's an example of where the personal pronoun is useful:

Are they leaving?	*Gidiyorlar mı?*
No, *we're* leaving.	*Hayır, biz gidiyoruz.*

'Understood' Verbs

Some sentences can have understood, unstated verbs:

We're Australians.	*Avustralyalıyız.*
	'Australia-of-(are)-we'.
They (are)(the ones) off the train.	*Trendenler.*
	'Train-from-they'.

Negative

To form the negative, put the suffix *-me(z)-*, *-ma(z)-* after the verb root and before any other suffixes; there may be a *y* added as a buffer:

to come – *gelmek*	not to come – *gelmemek*
I came – *geldim*	I didn't come – *gelmezdim*
I'll go – *gideceğim*	I won't go – *gitmeyeceğim*

To make a negative in sentences with an unstated, 'understood' verb, use the word *değil*, 'not', where the verb would be.

This place is not comfortable.	*Burası rahat değil.* 'This-place-comfortable-not'.
It's not expensive.	*Pahalı değil.* 'Expensive not'.

Questions

To form a question, add the suffix *-mi, -mı, -mu, -mü* (depending on vowel harmony) at the very end of the verb. Though the suffix is part of the same word, a space is customarily left in front of it.

The bus is coming.
    Otobüs geliyor.
Is the bus coming?
    Otobüs geliyor mu?

Greetings & Civilities

Ottoman etiquette was complex, graceful and flowery, with all sorts of polite words and phrases. Today Turks are much more informal, but vestiges of Ottoman politeness remain. If you visit a Turk's home, you will be shown to the best seat in the room, welcomed formally, offered sweets, cigarettes and tea or coffee, and expected to exchange pleasantries for a few minutes. On an intercity bus ride, the *yardımcı* (bus driver's assistant) will come through the bus with a bottle of lemon cologne and shake some into your hands so that you can refresh your face and neck. They still offer sweets before takeoff on Turkish Airlines flights, not just to help your ears adjust to altitude, but as a welcoming symbol of Turkish hospitality as well.

Greetings
Use a greeting whenever you approach someone. The all-purpose informal greeting, *merhaba* (hello), is good in any situation, with

anyone, at any time of day. Muslims in the more traditional towns may say *salaam aleikum* (peace be with you), but they usually only say it to other Muslims. The correct response is *aleikum salaam* (and with you, peace).

To get someone's attention, whether a man, woman or group of people, say *efendim*. With a child you can use *çocuk* (child). Ticket-takers on buses or ferryboats may use *evet* (yes) to get your attention so they can check your tickets. If you bump someone inadvertently, say *affedersiniz* (pardon me). You can also get away with simply saying *pardon* (pahr-DOHN).

Turks will welcome you into a shop or a restaurant, offer you a seat, a cigarette or anything at all using the word *buyurun(uz)*, which means 'be my guest' or 'help yourself'. The closest equivalent in another language is the German politeness-word 'bitte'. You'll hear *buyurun* a lot, and sometimes the plural/extra-polite *buyurunuz*. You can use it yourself if you offer an elderly person your seat on the bus or offer food, etc to someone.

Turks may assume that you're German and greet you with 'guten tag'– many Turks who were formerly 'guest-workers' in Germany do speak German, but many know little more than this greeting.

Sir! Miss! Madam! Ladies and gentlemen!	*Efendim!* eh-FEHN-deem
Hi! Hello!	*Merhaba!* MEHR-hah-bah
good morning/good day	*günaydın* gur-na-y-DUHN
good evening	*iyi akşamlar* ee-YEE ahk-shahm-LAHR

How are you?	*Nasılsınız?* NAHS-suhl-suh-nuhz
Very well, thank you.	*Çok iyiyim, teşekkür ederim.* CHOHK ee-YEE-yeem tesh-eh-KEUR eh-deh-reem
And how are you?	*Siz nasılsınız?* SEEZ nahs-suhl-suh-nuhz
Come on in! Help yourself! ('I offer you this!')	*Buyurun(uz)!* BOOY-roon(-ooz)

Goodbyes

good night	*iyi geceler* ee-YEE geh-jeh-LEHR
goodbye (person leaving)	*allaha ısmarladık* ah-LAHS-mahr-lah-duhk
bon voyage/goodbye (person staying)	*güle güle* gur-LEH gur-LEH
Let's go!	*Gidelim!* gee-deh-LEEM

Civilities

yes	*evet* eh-VEHT
no	*hayır* HAH-yuhr
there's none/it doesn't exist/no	*yok* YOHK
I/we have it/it exists/there is	*var* VAHR
please	*lütfen* LURT-fehn

thankyou (formal)	*teşekkür ederim* tesh-eh-KEUR eh-deh-reem
thanks (informal)	*teşekkürler* tesh-eh-keur-LEHR
thanks (informal)	*sağ ol* or *sağ olun* SOWL or SAAH ohl-loon
you're welcome	*bir şey değil* beer SHEY deh-YEEL
of course	*tabii* tah-BEE
pardon me	*affedersiniz* AF-feh-DEHR-see-neez
You've gone to a lot of trouble.	*Çok zahmet ettiniz.* CHOKE zahh-MEHT eht-tee-neez

Body Language

Turks indicate 'yes' by nodding the head once, forward and down. They may also say *var* ('we have it' – more literally 'it exists') the same way. To indicate 'no' in Turkey, nod your head up and

back, lifting your eyebrows at the same time – simply raising your eyebrows also signifies 'no'. Remember, when Turks seem to be giving you an arch look, they are often only saying 'no'. They may also make the sound 'tsk', which also means 'no'.

Wagging your head from side to side doesn't mean 'no' in Turkish, it means 'I don't understand'. So if a Turk asks you, 'Are you looking for the bus to Ankara?' and you shake your head, he or she will assume you don't understand English and will probably ask you the same question again, this time in German.

There are other body-language signs that can cause confusion, especially when you're out shopping. For instance, if you want to indicate length ('I want a fish this big'), don't hold your hands apart at the desired length; rather hold out your arm and place a flat hand on it, measuring from your fingertips to the hand. Thus, if you want a pretty big fish, you must 'chop' your arm with your other hand at about the elbow.

Height is indicated by holding a flat hand the desired distance above the floor or some other flat surface such as a counter or table top.

Turks will invite you to follow them by waving one of their hands downward and toward themselves in a scooping motion. Some Turks, particularly women, will hold their hand in the same way, but flutter their fingers instead of scooping. Both signs mean 'follow me'. Wiggling an upright finger would never occur to a Turk, except perhaps as a vaguely obscene gesture.

Polite Phrases

Besides the normal everyday pleasantries such as 'hello' and 'thankyou', on certain occasions Turks will automatically hold forth with a special phrase appropriate to the occasion. When you sit down to a meal, it's *Afiyet olsun!* (May it contribute to your health!). If you have suffered illness or injury, or if you have a sudden and very troubling problem, the appropriate phrase is *Geçmiş olsun!* (May it be in your past!) The giveaway in these phrases is the last word *...olsun* (Let it be (that)...). If you hear it, and the context seems right, just say *sağ ol* (thanks) in response.

May it contribute to your health! (said to someone sitting down to a meal)
   Afiyet olsun!
      ah-fee-EHT ohl-soon

May your life be spared! (said to someone who has just experienced a death in the family)
   Başınız sağ olsun!
      bah-shuh-nuhz SAAH ohl-soon

May your soul be safe from harm! (said to someone who has just accidentally broken something)
   Canınız sağ olsun!
      JAH-nuh-nuhz SAAH ohl-soon

May it be in your past! (said to someone who is ill, injured or otherwise distressed)
   Geçmiş olsun!
      gech-MEESH ohl-soon

May it last for hours! (said to someone who just emerged from a bath or shower, a shave or a hair cut. It's a corruption of *Sıhhatler olsun!* (May it keep you healthy!)
   Saatler olsun!
      saaht-LEHR ohl-soon

Health to your hand! (said to a cook who has prepared a delicious meal)
Elinize sağlık!
   el-lee-nee-ZEH saah-LUHK

In your honour! or To your health! (toast when drinking)
Şerefinize!
   sheh-REH-fee-nee-ZEH

Forms of Address

In Ottoman times, the hierarchy of forms of address had many levels. However, the only Ottoman forms of address you're likely to run into are *Bey* (Mr) and *Hanım* (Ms), preceded by a person's first name, as in *Mehmet Bey* or *Ayşe Hanım*. Women have never been separated into 'Miss' and 'Mrs' in Turkish; there was and is only 'Ms', even under the Ottomans. The Ottoman form of address is the one commonly used in most situations today, so you will usually address people as *Ahmet Bey* or *Perihan Hanım*. Just to use a person's name with no title is very informal, and is impolite if you don't know the person well.

The romantic old word *Efendi* is not used much anymore; in fact it is now used only to indicate someone of very low social position. The dustman may be *Hasan Efendi*, but the higher-status driver of the rubbish truck is *Ahmet Bey*. You should not use *Efendi* at all. Note that *Efendim* is the polite, completely acceptable non-specific form of address for men and women, singly or in a group – just be sure to add that *m*!

Under Atatürk's republic, the Turkish Language Society introduced the 'pure Turkish' forms of address *Bay* (Mr) and *Bayan* (Ms) followed by the family name: eg *Bay Kocatürk* (Mr Kocatürk) or *Bayan Kocatürk* (Ms Kocatürk). These are used in more formal situations: in addressing envelopes, in television interviews and game shows, by government officials, on official forms, etc. You may find yourself being addressed this way occasionally.

It is also common to use a job title followed by *Bey* or *Hanım* instead of the person's given name. This is useful because in many situations you'll know the person's job or title but not their name.

'Mr Official' (police or civil)	*Memur Bey* meh-MOOR bey
'Ms Director'	*Müdür Hanım* mew-DEUR hah-nuhm
'Mr Driver' (taxi or bus)	*Şoför Bey* shoh-FUR bey
'Mr Doctor, Ms Doctor'	*Doktor Bey, Doktor Hanım* dohk-TOHR bey, dohk-TOHR hanuhm
'Mr Waiter'	*Garson Bey* gahr-SOHN bey
'Mr Conductor' (Ticket-Taker)	*Biletçi Bey* bee-LEHT-chee bey

Small Talk

Even though tourists are now a common sight in Turkey, many Turks will still be curious about you, where you come from and how you are enjoying their country. In hotel lobbies, on bus and train trips, in cafés and teahouses, you may be greeted, offered cigarettes and tea, and engaged in conversation.

Nationalities

Where are you from?

Nerelisiniz?
NEH-reh-lee-see-neez

I'm an Australian.

Avustralyalıyım.
AH-voo-STRAHL-yah-L
UH-yuhm

I'm from England.	*İngiltereliyim.* EEN-geel-TEH-reh-LEE-yeem
I'm English.	*İngilizim.* EEN-gee-LEE-zeem
I'm from America.	*Amerikalıyım.* ah-MEH-ree-kah-LUH-yuhm
I'm Canadian.	*Kanadalıyım.* KAH-nah-dah-LUH-yuhm

Note: the following are the words for nationalities, not languages. 'French language', for example, is *Fransızca*, while a 'French person' is *Fransız*.

France	*Fransa* FRAHN-sa
French	*Fransız* frahn-SUHZ
Germany	*Almanya* al-MAHN-ya
German	*Alman* al-MAHN
Israel	*İsrail* EE-sra-YEEL
Israeli	*İsrailli* EE-srah-yeel-LEE
Italy	*İtalya* ee-TAHL-ya

Italian	*İtalyalı/İtalyan* ee-TAHL-yah-LUH/ee-tahl-YAHN
Japan	*Japon/Japonya* zha-POHN/zha-POHN-yah
Japanese	*Japon/Japonyalı* zha-POHN/zha-POHN-yah-LUH
Spain	*İspanya* ee-SPAHN-yah
Spanish	*İspanyol* ee-spahn-YOHL
Sweden	*İsveç* ee-SVETCH
Swedish	*İsveçli* ee-svetch-LEE
Switzerland	*İsviçre* ee-SVEETCH-reh
Swiss	*İsviçreli* ee-SVEETCH-reh-LEE
Turkey	*Türkiye* TEWR-kee-yeh
Turkish	*Türk* TEWRK

Small Talk

What's your name?	*Adınız ne?* or *İsminiz ne?* AH-duh-NUHZ neh, EES-mee-NEEZ neh
My name's Julia.	*İsmim Julia.* eess-MEEM Julia

Is this your first visit to Turkey?

Türkiye'ye ilk defa mı geliyorsunuz?
TEUR-kee-yeh-yeh EELK deh-fah muh geh-lee-yohr-soo-nooz

How do you like Turkey?

Türkiye'yi nasıl buluyorsunuz?
TEUR-kee-yeh-yee NAH-suhl boo-loo-yohr-soo-nooz

Are you married?

Evli misiniz?
ev-LEE-mee-see-neez

I'm married/I'm not married.

Evliyim/Evli değilim.
ehv-LEE-yeem/ehv-LEE deh-YEEL-eem

Do you have children?

Çocuk var mı?
choh-jook VAHR muh

No, none.

Hayır, yok.
HAH-yuhr, YOHK

No, I have no children.

Hayır, çocuğum yok.
HAH-yuhr, choh-JOO-uhm YOHK

Yes, a daughter and a son.

Evet, bir kız ve bir oğul.
eh-VEHT, beer KUHZ veh beer oh-OOL

How old are you?

Kaç yaşındasınız?
KAHTCH yah-shun-dah-suh-nuhz

I'm 25.

Yirmibeş yaşındayım.
YEER-mee-BESH yah-shuhn-dah-yuhm

Occupations

What's your job?

Ne iş yaparsınız?
  NEH eesh yah-pahr-suh-NUHZ

I'm a businessman/business-woman.

İşadamım/İşkadınım
  EESH ah-dah-muhm/EESH-kah-duh-nuhm

I'm a doctor.

Doktorum.
  dohk-TOHR-room

I'm an engineer.

Mühendisim.
  mur-hehn-DEE-seem

I'm a musician.

Müzisyenim/Müzikçiyim.
  mur-zee-SYEH-NEEM/mur-zeek- CHEE-yeem

I'm a student.	*Öğrenciyim.* UR-rehn-JEE-yeem
I'm a teacher.	*Öğretmenim.* UR-reht-MEHN-eem
I'm a journalist.	*Gazeteciyim.* GAHZ-teh-JEE-yeem
I'm a (factory) worker.	*İşçiyim.* eesh-CHEE-yeem
I'm a nurse.	*Hemşireyim.* HEM-shee-REH-yeem

Religions

Are you a ...?	*... mısınız?* huh-REES-tee-YAHN muh-suh-nuhz
Christian	*Hristiyan* huh-REES-tee-YAHN
Buddhist	*Budist* boo-DEEST mee-see-neez
Catholic	*Katolik* KAH-toh-LEEK mee- see-neez
Jew	*Musevi* MOO-seh-VEE mee-see- neez
Muslim	*Müslüman* mur-slur-MAHN-muh- suh-nuhz
Protestant	*Protestan* PROH-tess-TAHN muh- suh-nuhz

Feelings

To express most feelings, add the suffix *-im*, *-ım*, *-um*, or *-üm*, depending on vowel harmony, to an adjective. To say 'we're...', add the suffix *-iz*, *-ız*, *-uz*, or *-üz*.

I'm tired.	*Yorgunum.*
	yohr-GOON-oom
We're tired.	*Yorgunuz.*
	yohr-GOON-ooz
I'm hungry.	*Açım.*
	AH-chuhm
We're thirsty.	*Susuzuz.*
	soo-SOOZ-ooz
I'm happy.	*Mutluyum.*
	moot-LOO-yoom
I'm angry.	*Kızgınım.*
	kuhz-GUHN-uhm
We're sorry.	*Üzgünüz.*
	urz-GURN-urz

Some feelings are expressed by idioms:

I'm sleepy. (my sleep has come)	*Uykum geldi.*
	ooy-KOOM gehl-dee

Accommodation

Turkey has all classes of accommodation, from student dormitories and little family-run pensions to international-class luxury hotels. Some Turks will assume that, as a foreigner, you'll want to stay at a four-star place. But when you ask them for directions to a good, cheap hotel they'll readily oblige and recommend a place where they would stay.

Finding Accommodation

Where is …?	*… nerede?* NEH-reh-deh
a hotel?	*bir otel* BEER oh-TEHL
Where is a clean, cheap hotel?	*Ucuz, temiz bir otel nerede?* oo-JOOZ teh-MEEZ beer oh-TEHL NEH-reh-deh
I want a room for only 20,000 liras.	*Yalnız yirmi bin lira için bir* *oda istiyorum.* YAHL-nuhz YEER-mee been LEE-rah ee-cheen beer OH-dah eess-tee-yoh-room

At the Hotel

Even in the smallest hotels and pensions there will probably be someone who speaks a few words of English. When there's not, to request a room, say one or more of the following phrases, adding … *istiyorum* (I want …), or … *istiyoruz* for the plural (we want …). For example, *iki kişilik oda istiyorum* (I want a two-person

35

room), or *çift yataklı bir oda istiyorum* (I want a twin-bed room). For the courageous, try this: *sakin iki kişilik geniş yataklı banyosuz bir oda istiyoruz* (We want a quiet, bathless double room with a wide (double) bed).

Checking In

I/we want a ...	*Bir ... istiyorum/istiyoruz.*
	BEER ... eess-tee-yoh-room
bed	*yatak*
	yah-TAHK
room	*oda*
	OH-dah
single room	*kişilik oda*
	kee-shee-leek OH-dah

double room	*iki kişilik oda*
	ee-KEE kee-shee-leek OH-dah
triple room	*üç kişilik oda*
	URCH kee-shee-leek OH-dah
room with one bed	*tek yataklı oda*
	TEHK yah-tahk-LUH OH-dah
room with two beds	*iki yataklı oda*
	ee-KEE yah-tahk-LUH OH-dah
room with twin beds	*çift yataklı oda*
	CHEEFT yah-tahk-LUH OH-dah
double bed	*geniş yatak*
	geh-NEESH yah-tahk
room with bath	*banyolu oda*
	BAHN-yoh-LOO oh-dah
room without bath	*banyosuz oda*
	BAHN-yoh-SOOZ oh-dah
room with shower	*duşlu oda*
	doosh-LOO oh-dah
room with washbasin	*lavabolu oda*
	LAH-vah-boh-LOO oh-dah
quiet room	*sakin bir oda*
	sah-KEEN beer oh-dah

Some Useful Words & Phrases

How much per night?
Bir gecelik ne kadar?
  BEER geh-jeh-leek NEH
  kah-dahr

Don't you have anything cheaper?
Hiç daha ucuz yok mu?
  HEETCH dah-HAH oo-JOOZ YOHK moo

That's too expensive.
Çok pahalı.
  CHOHK pah-hah-luh

Could I see the room?
Odayı görebilir miyim?
  OH-dah-yuh gur-reh-bee-LEER-mee-yeem

It's too small.
Çok küçük.
  chohk kur-churk

It's very noisy.
Çok gürültülü.
  'CHOKE' gur-rurl-tur-lur

How many liras?
Kaç lira?
  KAHCH lee-rah

Is there a cheaper (room)?
Daha ucuzu var mı?
  dah-HAH oo-jooz-oo VAHR muh

Is there a better (room)?
Daha iyisi var mı?
  dah-HAH ee-yee-see VAHR muh

included
dahil
  dah-HEEL

excluded
hariç
  hah-REECH

It's very expensive.
Çok pahalı.
  'CHOKE' pah-hah-luh

Is the tax included?	*Vergi dahil mi?*
	VEHR-gee dah-HEEL mee
Where is the toilet?	*Tuvalet nerede?*
	too-vah-LEHT neh-reh-deh?
Is a hot shower included?	*Sıcak duş dahil mi?*
	suh-JAHK DOOSH dah-HEEL mee
How much is a hot shower?	*Sıcak duş kaç lira?*
	suh-JAHK DOOSH KAHCH lee-rah
Where is the manager?	*Patron nerede?*
	pah-TROHN neh-reh-deh?
Where is someone who knows English?	*Ingilizce bilen bir kimse nerede?*
	EEN-geh-LEEZ-jeh bee-lehn beer KEEM-seh NEH-reh-deh?
It's fine, I'll take it.	*İyi, tutuyorum.*
	ee-YEE, too-too-YOH-room
It won't do.	*Olmuyor.*
	OHL-moo-yohr

Meals

Is breakfast included?	*Kahvaltı dahil mi?*
	KAHH-vahl-TUH dah-HEEL mee
Are meals included?	*Yemekler dahil mi?*
	yeh-mehk-LEHR dah-HEEL mee

I don't want to take meals.	*Yemekler istemiyorum.* yeh-mehk-LEHR eess-TEH-mee-yoh-room
Taking meals is required.	*Yemekler almak mecbur(dur).* yeh-mehk-LEHR ahl-mahk medj-BOOR(door)

Alternatives

Can I (we) sleep on the roof?	*Çatıda yatabilir miyim (miyiz)?* CHAH-tuh-DAH yah-tah-bee-LEER-mee-yeem (mee-yeez)
Can I (we) camp in the garden?	*Bahçede kamp yapabilir miyim (miyiz)?* BAHH-cheh-deh KAHMP yah-pah-bee-LEER mee-yeem (mee-yeez)
I (we) have a tent.	*Çadırım(ız) var.* CHAH-duhr-RUHM(-UHZ) vahr

I'll (we'll) be staying …	…*kalacağım (kalacağız)*
	kah-lah-jah-um
one night	*bir gece*
	BEER geh-jeh
two nights	*iki gece*
	ee-KEE geh-jeh
three nights	*üç gece*
	URCH geh-jeh
a few nights	*bir kaç gece*
	beer KAHTCH geh-jeh
(at least) a week	*(en azından) bir hafta*
	(EHN ah-zuhn-dahn) BEER
	hahf-tah
I'm not sure (how long I'm staying).	*henüz bilmiyorum.*
	HEH-nurz BEEL mee-yoh-room

Checking Out

I'm (we're) checking out …	… *gidiyorum (gidiyoruz).*
	gee-dee-yoh-room (-rooz)
now	*şimdi*
	SHEEM-dee
midday	*oğleye doğru*
	ur-leh-YEH doh-roo
this evening	*bu akşam*
	BOO ahk-SHAHM
tomorrow	*yarın*
	YAH-ruhn

Can I leave my stuff with you until ...?	*Bagajımı ... kadar sizinle bırakabilir miyim?* bah-GAZH-uh-muh ... kah-dahr see-ZEEN-leh
3 o'clock	*saat üçe* sah-AHT ur-CHEH
this afternoon	*oğleden sonraya* ur-leh-DEHN sohn-rah-YAH
this evening	*akşama* ahk-shah-MAH
Could I have the bill?	*Hesabım lütfen.* heh-SAH-buhm lurt-fehn

Getting Around

Turks are passionate travellers. The intercity-bus network operated by private companies is possibly the busiest in the world. Big, comfortable, modern buses shuttle between cities frequently, even if the cities are at opposite ends of the country. Minibuses serve the shorter routes. Some of the trains operated by the Turkish State Railways are very fast and comfortable, and like the buses, train fares are surprisingly cheap. Turkish Airlines has a useful schedule of flights, and competition is increasingly provided by smaller airlines.

You will undoubtedly do some of your Turkish travelling by bus. Though most cities have modern bus stations, some still have only collections of bus ticket offices, often near the market. Turkish bus stations, whether modern or not, are often very busy, and seemingly chaotic. At any city bus station, agents will approach you and ask where you want to go, then lead you to the ticket counter of a bus company operating buses to that destination. The agents do not expect tips, and they are not con men. But their company's bus may or may not be the next departure for your destination. It's good to check around on your own and ask about departure times before buying your ticket.

Where is a/the ...? ... *nerede?*
    NEH-reh-deh

  railway station *gar/istasyon*
    GAHR/ees-tah-SYOHN

  bus station *otogar*
    OH-toh-gahr

airport	*havaalanı*
	hah-VAH-ah-lah-nuh
boat/ship dock	*iskele*
	eess-KEH-leh
ticket office	*bilet satış ofisi*
	bee-LEHT sah-TUSH
	oh-fee-see
checkroom	*emanetçi*
	EH-mah-NEHT-chee

I want a ticket to …   … *bir bilet istiyorum.*
                              BEER bee-LEHT eess-tee-
                              yohr-room

How many liras is a ticket to ...?	*... bir bilet kaç lira?* beer bee-leht KAHCH lee-rah
Istanbul	*İstanbul'a* uh-STAHN-boo-LAH
Edirne	*Edirne'ye* eh-DEER-neh-YEH
Does this bus/train go to Izmir?	*Bu otobüs/tren İzmir'e gider mi?* BOO oh-toh-burss/trehn EEZ-meer-EH gee-DEHR mee
When does the bus to Ankara depart?	*Ankara'ya giden otobüs ne zaman kalkar?* AHN-kah-rah-YAH gee-dehn oh-toh-burss NEH zah-mahn kahl-kahr
When does it depart?	*Ne zaman kalkar?* NEH zah-mahn kahl-kahr
When does it arrive?	*Ne zaman gelir?* NEH zah-mahn geh-leer
Is there an earlier/later one?	*Daha erken/geç var mı?* dah-HAH ehr-kehn/getch VAHR muh
How many hours is the journey?	*Yolculuk kaç saat?* YOHL-joo-look KAHCH saa-AHT

Directions & Instructions

here	*burada*
	BOO-rah-dah
there	*şurada*
	SHOO-rah-dah
over there	*orada*
	OH-rah-dah
It's nearby/far away.	*Yakın/Uzak.*
	yah-KUHN/oo-ZAHK
Is it nearby/far away?	*Yakın mı?/Uzak mı?*
	yah-KUHN muh/oo-ZAHK
	muh
You can go on foot.	*Yürüyerek gidebilirsiniz.*
	yewr-ruy-yeh-REHK gee-
	deh-bee-leer-see-neez
Go straight ahead.	*Doğru gidin.*
	doh-ROO gee-deen
To the left/right.	*Sola/sağa.*
	soh-LAH/saah-AH

Let's go!	*Gidelim!*
	GEE-deh-LEEM
I'm in a hurry.	*Acelem var.*
	AH-jeh-LEHM vahr
Slow down!	*Yavaş gidin!*
	yah-VAHSH gee-deen
Stop (here)!	*(Burada) durun!*
	(BOO-rah-dah) DOO-roon
Wait here!	*Burada bekleyin!*
	BOO-rah-dah bek-leh-yeen

Some Useful Words & Phrases

map	*harita*
	HAH-ree-TAH
timetable	*tarife*
	TAH-ree-FEH
ticket	*bilet*
	bee-LEHT
reserved seat (numbered place)	*numaralı yer*
	noo-MAH-rah-LUH yehr
1st class	*birinci mevki/sınıf*
	beer-EEN-jee mehv-kee/ suh-nuhf
2nd class	*ikinci mevki/sınıf*
	ee-KEEN-jee mehv-kee/ suh-nuhf
single/one way	*gidiş*
	gee-DEESH
return/round trip	*gidiş-dönüş*
	gee-DEESH-dur-NURSH

student (ticket)	*öğrenci* or *talebe (bileti)*
	EWR-rehn-JEE, tah-leh-BEH
for today	*bugün için*
	BOO-gurn ee-cheen
for tomorrow	*yarın için*
	YAH-ruhn ee-cheen
for Friday ('Friday-day')	*cuma günü için*
	joo-MAH gur-nur ee-cheen
daily	*hergün*
	HEHR-gurn
arrival	*geliş/varış*
	geh-LEESH/vah-RUSH
departure	*gidiş/kalkış*
	gee-DEESH/kahl-KUHSH

Air

Will you please check this luggage?	*Bu bagaj kaydeder misiniz?*
	BOO bah-gazh kah-yeed-eh-DEHR mee-see-neez
airplane	*uçak*
	oo-CHAHK
airport	*havaalanı*
	hah-VAH-ah-lah-nuh
boarding pass	*biniş kartı*
	bee-NEESH kahr-tuh
customs	*gümrük*
	gurm-RURK
flight	*uçuş*
	oo-CHOOSH

gate ('door')	*kapı*
	kah-PUH
gate number one/two	*bir/iki numaralı çıkış kapısı*
	BEER/ee-KEE noo-mah-rah-LUH chuh-KUSH kah-puh-suh
security check	*güvenlik kontrolü*
	gur-vehn-LEEK khon-troh-lur

Bus

bus	*otobüs*
	oh-toh-BURSS
bus terminal	*otogar*
	OH-toh-gahr
direct (bus)	*direk(t)*
	dee-REK
indirect (route)	*aktarmalı*
	ahk-tahr-mah-LUH

Train

railway	*demiryolu*
	deh-MEER-yoh-loo
train	*tren*
	TREHN
railway station	*gar/istasyon*
	GAHR/ees-tahs-YOHN
sleeping car	*yataklı vagon*
	yah-tahk-LUH vah-gohn
dining car	*yemekli vagon*
	yeh-mehk-LEE vah-gohn

couchette
kuşet
koo-SHEHT

no-smoking car
sigara içilmeyen vagon
see-GAH-rah ee-CHEEL-
mee-yehn vah-gohn

Boat

berth
yatak
yah-TAHK

cabin
kamara
KAH-mah-rah

class
mevki/sınıf
MEHV-kee/suh-NUHF

dock
iskele
eess-KEH-leh

ferryboat
feribot
FEH-ree-boht

port tax
liman vergisi
lee-MAHN vehr-gee-see

ship
gemi
geh-MEE

Road

air (for tyres)
hava (lastik)
hah-VAH (laass-TEEK)

auto electric repairman
oto elektrikçi
oh-TOH ee-lehk-TREEK-
chee

brake(s)
fren
FREHN

Careful! Slow!	*Dikkat! Yavaş!* deek-KAHT, yah-VAHSH
climbing lane	*tırmanma şeridi* tuhr-MAHN-mah sheh-ree-dee
headlamp	*far* FAHR
highways	*karayolları* KAH-rah-yoh-lah-ruh
long vehicle	*uzun araç* oo-ZOON ah-rahch
lubrication	*yağlama* YAH-lah-MAH
motor oil	*motor yağı* moh-TOHR yah-uh

motorway/expressway	*otoyol* OH-toh-yohl
normal/regular	*normal* nohr-MAHL
petrol/gasoline	*benzin* behn-ZEEN
road construction	*yol yapımı* YOHL yah-puh-muh
road repairs	*yol onarımı* YOHL oh-NAH-ruh-muh
super/extra	*süper* sur-PEHR
tyre repairman	*oto lastikçi* oh-TOH laass-TEEK-chee
(car) washing	*yıkama* yuh-kah-MAH
wide vehicle	*geniş araç* geh-NEESH ah-rahch

Around Town

Addresses

Addresses in Turkish cities are often given in the form of directions:

Cumhuriyet Caddesi Sepetçi Sokak No. 23/5, Gülistan Ap. 3. Kat, Taksim.

In the Taksim neighbourhood, take Republic Ave (main thoroughfare), to Basketmaker's St (side street) and look for building number 23 (the Rose Garden Apartments), then go to apartment 5 on the 3rd floor.

If you stand in the street looking puzzled for a few seconds, some helpful person is sure to approach you and ask if you need help finding an address.

Where is …?	*… nerede?*
	NEH-reh-deh
the Hacibaba Restaurant	*Hacibaba Lokantası*
	hah-JUH-bah-bah loh-KAHN-tah-suh
the (main) post office	*(merkez) postane*
	(mehr-KEHZ) POHSS-tah-neh
a police officer	*polis memuru*
	poh-LEES meh-moo-roo

the Australian Embassy

Avustralya büyükelçiliği
   AH-voos-TRAHL-yah
   bur-YURK ehl-chee-lee-
   ee

the Turkish bath

hamam
   hah-MAHM

At the Post Office

I would like an air-mail
   stamp for a postcard to
   Australia.

*Avustralya'ya uçakla kartpos-
tal için bir pul rica ederim.*
   AH-voo-STRAHL-yah-yah
   oo-CHAHK-lah KAHRT-
   poss-TAHL ee-cheen beer
   POOL ree-JAH eh-deh-
   reem

How many liras (to send this) to Canada?	*Kanada'ya kaç lira?* KAH-nah-dah-yah KAHCH lee-rah
Is there a letter for me in poste restante?	*Postrestanda bana mektup var mı?* POHST-ress-TAHN-dah bah-NAH mek-toop VAHR muh

Some Useful Words

aerogramme	*hava mektubu/aerogram* hah-VAH mek-too-boo/EHR-oh-grahm
air mail	*uçakla/uçak ile* oo-CHAHK-lah/oo-CHA HK-ee-leh
customs	*gümrük* gurm-RURK
express mail/special delivery	*ekspres* ehks-PRESS
facsimile	*elektronik mektup/fax* eh-LEK-troh-NEEK mehk-toop/FAHKS
letter	*mektup* mehk-TOOP
money order	*havale* hah-vah-LEH
parcel	*koli/paket* KOH-lee/pah-KEHT

post office	*postane/postahane* POHSS-tah-NEH/POHS-tah-hah-neh
post-telephone-telegraph	*PTT* peh-teh-TEH
postage stamp	*pul* POOL
postcard	*kartpostal* KAHRT-pohs-TAHL
poste restante/general delivery	*postrestant* pohst-rehs-TAHNT
registered mail	*kayıtlı* KAH-yuht-luh
telephone debit card	*telekart* TEH-leh-kahrt
telephone token	*jeton* zheh-TOHN

At the Bank

Not all bank branch offices have exchange facilities. If a branch does not, a bank officer will point you toward a branch that does. Sometimes the exchange desk is one flight up from the main floor. Always take your passport when changing money, and hold onto your exchange slips so that you can change unused liras back into your own currency.

Note that most post offices will change foreign currency notes (but not travellers' cheques) into Turkish liras.

Do you accept these travellers' cheques?	*Bu seyahat çekleri kabul eder misiniz?*
	BOO seh-yah-HAHT chek-leh-ree KAH-bool eh-DEHR mee-see-neez
Do you accept Eurocheques?	*Euroçek kabul eder misiniz?*
	UHR-roh-chek KAH-bool eh-DEHR mee-see-neez
Would you change this?	*Bunu bozar mısınız?*
	boo-NOO boh-ZAHR muh-suh-nuhz

Some Useful Words

cash	*efektif*
	eh-fehk-TEEF
cashier	*kasa/vezne*
	KAH-sah/VEHZ-neh
cheque	*çek*
	CHEK
coin(s)	*madeni para*
	mah-deh-NEE pah-rah
commission (fee)	*komisyon*
	koh-mees-YOHN
exchange rate	*kur*
	KOOR
(currency) exchange	*kambiyo*
	KAHM-bee-yoh
foreign currency	*döviz*
	dur-VEEZ
money	*para*
	PAH-rah

paper money	*kağıt para*
	kyaah-UHT pah-rah
purchase	*alış*
	ah-LUSH
sale	*veriş*
	veh-REESH
small change	*bozuk para*
	boh-ZOOK pah-rah
tax	*vergi*
	VEHR-gee

Bureaucracy

Turkish official bureaucracy has a well-deserved reputation for slowness and abundant frowns. A bureaucrat's favourite word is *Olmaz!* (Impossible!). Still, as a foreigner you will probably be given special consideration and perhaps even a smile. Bribes are rarely asked of foreigners, and you should not suggest one. Be patient with the creeping wheels of bureaucracy, and above all do not lose your temper.

official (person)	*memur*
	meh-MOOR
director	*müdür*
	mew-DEWR
document	*belge*
	BEHL-geh
form	*forma*
	FOHR-mah
Wait!	*Bekleyin!*
	behk-LEH-yeen
tomorrow	*yarın*
	YAHR-uhn

Emergencies

Help!	*İmdat!*
	eem-DAHT
Watch out!	*Dikkat!*
	deek-KAHT
Thief!	*Hırsız!*
	huhr-SUHZ
(There's a) fire!	*Yangın var!*
	yahn-GUHN vahr

There's been an accident.

Bir kaza oldu.
  beer kah-ZAH ohl-doo

Call ('tell') the police!

Polise haber verin!
  POH-lees-SEH hah-BEHR
  veh-reen

Call an ambulance/a doctor!

*Bir cankurtaran/doktor
çağırın!*
  beer-JAHN-koor-tah-rahn/
  dohk-TOHR chaa-uhr- uhn

In the Country

Weather

What's the weather report?	*Hava raporu nasıl?* hah-VAH rah-poh-roo nah-suhl
The weather will be hot/cold.	*Hava sıcak/soğuk olacak.* hah-VAH suh-JAHK/soh-OOK oh-lah-jahk
It's going to rain/snow.	*Yağmur/kar yağacak.* yah-MOOR/KAHR yah-ah-jahk
The weather is beautiful today.	*Bugün hava güzel.* BUR-gurn hah-VAH gur-ZEHL

Some Useful Words

autumn	*son bahar* SOHN bah-hahr
cloud(y)	*bulut(lu)* boo-LOOT(-LOO)
freeze (verb)	*donmak* dohn-MAHK
ice	*buz* BOOZ
'Indian summer'	*pastırma yazı* pahss-TUHR-mah yah-zuh
rain (noun)	*yağmur* yaah-MOOR

61

rain (verb)	*yağmur yağmak*
	yaah-MOOR yaah-mahk
snow (noun)	*kar*
	KAHR
spring	*ilk bahar*
	EELK bah-hahr
summer	*yaz*
	YAHZ
sun	*güneş*
	gur-NEHSH
weather ('air')	*hava*
	hah-VAH
wind	*rüzgar*
	rurz-GAHR
winter	*kış*
	KUHSH

Geographical Terms

beach	*plaj*
	PLAZH
cave	*mağara*
	MAAH-ah-rah
field	*tarla*
	TAHR-lah
harbour	*liman*
	lee-MAHN
hill	*tepe*
	TEH-peh
house	*ev*
	EHV

lake	*göl*
	GURL
mountain	*dağ*
	DAAH
mountaineer(ing)	*dağcı(lık)*
	DAAH-juh(LUHK)
mud	*çamur*
	chah-MOOR
river	*ırmak/nehir*
	uhr-MAHK/neh-HEER
road	*yol*
	YOHL
rock	*taş*
	TAHSH

sand	*kum* KOOM
sea	*deniz* deh-NEEZ
summit	*doruk/zirve* doh-ROOK/ZEER-veh
trail	*patika* PAH-tee-KAH
tree	*ağaç* aah-AHTCH
valley	*dere* DEH-reh
waterfall	*şelale* sheh-LAH-leh

Sights

bridge	*köprü* kur-PREW
church	*kilise* kee-LEE-seh
fortress	*kale/hisar* kah-LEH/hee-SAHR
historical/renowned	*tarihi* TAH-ree-HEE
mosque	*cami* JAH-mee
museum	*müze* mur-ZEH
old	*eski* ess-KEE

ruin(s)	*harabe(ler)* HAH-rah-BEH(-LEHR)
statue	*heykel* hey-KEL
temple	*tapınak/mabed* TAH-puh-NAHK/mah-BED

Village Life

village(r)	*köy(lü)* KURY(-LUR)
farmer	*çiftçi* CHEEFT-chee
crop/harvest	*ürün* ewr-RURHN

Animals

bull	*boğa* boh-AH
camel	*deve* DEH-veh
cat	*kedi* KEH-dee
cow	*inek* ee-NEHK

dog	*köpek*
	kur-PEHK
donkey	*eşek*
	eh-SHEK
duck	*ördek*
	ur-DEHK
goat	*keçi*
	KEH-chee
goose	*kaz*
	KAHZ
horse	*at*
	AHT
sheep/ram	*koyun/koç*
	koy-YOON/KOHCH
water buffalo	*manda*
	mahn-DAH
wolf	*kurt*
	KOORT

Insects & Pests

bug	*böcek*
	bur-JEHK
cockroach	*hamam böceği*
	hah-MAHM bur-jeh-yee
fly	*sinek*
	see-NEHK
mosquito	*sivrisinek*
	see-VREE-see-nehk
poison(ous)	*zehir(li)*
	zeh-HEER(-LEE)

scorpion	*akrep* ah-KREP
snake	*yılan* yuh-LAHN

Camping

Is there a camping place round here?	*Buralarda bir kamp yeri var mı?* BOO-rah-lahr-dah beer KAMP yeh-ree VAHR muh
Can I/we camp here?	*Burada kamp yapabilir miyim/miyiz?* BOO-rah-dah kahmp yah-pah-bee-LEER-mee-yeem/mee-yeez
Is one allowed to make a fire?	*Ateş yakmak serbest mi?* ah-TESH yahk-mahk sehr-BEST-mee
Where is the electric hookup?	*Elektrik bağlantısı nerede?* eh-lehk-TREEK baa-lahn-tuh-suh NEH-reh-deh
Where is the shower/toilet?	*Duş/tuvalet nerede?* DOOSH/too-vah-LEHT neh-reh-deh
Where can I have my gas cylinder filled?	*Gaz tüpümü nerede doldurabilirim?* GAHZ tur-pur-mur NEH-reh-deh dohl-doo-rah-bee-leer-eem

Some Useful Words

tent	*çadır*
	CHAH-duhr
caravan (trailer)	*karavan*
	KAH-rah-vahn
camping place	*kamp yeri*
	KAMP yeh-ree

Food

Turkish cuisine is based on lamb and mutton, but beef and chicken are also readily available. Though Muslims don't touch pork, you may occasionally find pork products offered at the fancier big-city and resort restaurants. Seafood is a Turkish specialty, and the Muslim prohibition against eating shellfish is ignored by many modern Turks. Wonderful fresh vegetables and fruits are a big part of the Turkish diet. In fact, the Turks have more than 40 ways of preparing eggplant; at least one of these is as a sweet dessert! Turkish bread is a delicious sourdough loaf baked fresh morning and afternoon. You can buy it by the loaf, half loaf, or even quarter loaf.

In a traditional workers' restaurant such as a *kebapçı*, *köfteci* or *pideci*, no alcoholic beverages are ever served, and the simple *lokanta* will observe this rule as well. But in slightly classier restaurants serving a variety of dishes, beer, wine, *rakı,* and other drinks are available.

If you don't eat meat, you can select from the many soups, vegetable dishes, *meze* plates, and salads available. But you should be aware that many Turkish soups and vegetable dishes are made using small quantities of meat as a flavouring.

Some Useful Words & Phrases

Is there a kebap restaurant *Buralarda bir kebapçı var mı?*
around here?   BOO-rah-LAHR-dah beer
    keh-BAHP-chuh VAHR muh

At your service!	*Buyurun(-uz)!*
	BOOY-roon(-ooz)
Come, look!	*Gelin, bakın!*
	GEH-leen, BAH-kuhn
Is/are there any ...?	*... var mı?*
	VAHR muh
shish kebap	*şiş kebap*
	SHEESH keh-bahp
appetizers	*meze*
	MEH-zeh
fresh fish	*taze balık*
	taa-ZEH bah-LUHK
wine	*şarap*
	shah-RAHP
meatless dishes	*etsiz yemekler*
	eht-SEEZ yeh-mehk-lehr
Please bring ...	*Lütfen ... getirin.*
	LURT-fehn geh-TEE-reen
water	*su*
	SOO
salad	*salata*
	sah-LAH-tah
salt and pepper	*tuz ve biber*
	TOOZ veh bee-BEHR

Vegetarians

I cannot eat ...	*... yiyemiyorum.*
	yee-YEH-mee-yoh-room
any meat	*hiç et*
	HEETCH EHT

eggs	*yumurta* YOO-moor-TAH
spicy peppers	*acı biber …* ah-JUH bee-behr
I do not even eat meat juices.	*Et suyu bile yiyemiyorum.* EHT soo-YOO bee-leh yee-YEH-mee-yoh-room
I eat chicken/fish.	*Tavuk/balık yiyorum.* tah-VOOK/bah-LUHK yee-yoh-room
I eat only fruit and vegetables.	*Yalnız meyve ve sebze yiyorum.* YAHL-nuhz mey-VEH ve seb-ZEH yee-yoh-room

Types of Restaurants

aileye mahsustur (ah-yee-leh-YEH mah-SOOS-toor) – a dining room reserved for couples and single women

büfe (bew-FEH) – a snack shop

fırın (FUH-ruhn) – a bakery (oven)

kebapçı (keh-BAHP-chuh) – a kebap (roast meat) shop

köfteci (KURF-teh-jee) – a köfte (meatball) shop

lokanta (loh-KAHN-tah) – a simple restaurant with ready food

pastane (PAHSS-tah-neh) – a pastry shop

pideci (PEE-deh-jee) – a Turkish-style pizza place
restaurant/restoran (REHSS-toh-RAHN) – fancier than a
  lokanta, usually serving alcohol

Meals

meal/dish of food	*yemek*
	yeh-MEHK
to eat	*yemek*
	yeh-MEHK
to eat a meal	*yemek yemek*
	yeh-MEHK yeh-mehk
breakfast	*kahvaltı*
	KAHH-vahl-TUH
lunch	*öğle yemeği*
	ury-LEH yeh-meh-yee
supper	*akşam yemeği*
	ahk-SHAHM yeh-meh-yee

Utensils

drinking glass	*bardak*
	bahr-DAHK
fork	*çatal*
	chah-TAHL
knife	*bıçak*
	buh-CHAHK
napkin	*peçete*
	PEH-cheh-TEH
plate	*tabak*
	tah-BAHK
spoon	*kaşık*
	kah-SHUHK

cup	*fincan* feen-JAHN

Soups

soup	*çorba* CHOHR-bah
broth with mutton	*haşlama* HAHSH-lah-MAH
chicken soup	*tavuk çorbası* tah-VOOK chor-bah-suh
egg-and-lemon ('wedding') soup	*düğün çorbası* dur-URN chor-bah-suh
lentil-and-rice soup	*ezo gelin çorbası* EH-zoh GEH-leen chor-bah-suh
lentil soup	*mercimek çorbası* mehr-jee-MEHK chor-bah-suh
mutton broth (with egg)	*et suyu (yumurtalı)* EHT soo-yoo (yoo-moor-tah-LUH)
tomato soup	*domates çorbası* doh-MAH-tess chohr-bah-suh
tripe soup	*işkembe çorbası* eesh-KEHM-beh chor-bah-suh
trotter soup	*paça* PAH-chah
vegetable soup	*sebze çorbası* SEHB-zeh chor-bah-suh

vermicelli soup	*şehriye çorbası*
	shehh-ree-YEH chor-bah-suh
yoghurt and barley soup	*yayla çorbası*
	YAY-lah chor-bah-suh

Appetisers

Turkish appetisers (*meze,* MEH-zeh) can include almost any-thing, and you can easily – and delightfully – make an entire meal of them. Often you will be brought a tray from which you can choose those you want.

beyaz peynir (bey-AHZ pey-neer) – white, sheep's milk cheese
börek (bur-REHK) – flaky pastry filled with white cheese or meat
cacık (jah-JUHK) – beaten yoghurt with grated cucumber and garlic
patlıcan salatası (paht-luh-JAHN sah-lah-tah-suh) – auber-gine/eggplant purée
pilaki/piyaz (pee-LAH-kee/pee-YAHZ) – cold white beans and onions vinaigrette
tarama salatası (tah-rah-MAH sah-lah-tah-suh) – red caviar in mayonnaise

Seafood

A menu is no use in ordering fish (*balık*). You must ask the waiter what's fresh, and then ask the price (*Kaç lira?*). The fish will be weighed and the price computed at the day's per-kg market rate. Sometimes you can haggle. Buy fish that are in season (*mevsimli*), as fish out of season are very expensive.

Aegean tuna	*trança*
	TRAHN-chah
anchovy (fresh)	*hamsi*
	HAHM-see
black bream	*karagöz*
	KAH-rah-gurz
bluefish	*lüfer*
	lur-FEHR
grey mullet	*kefal*
	keh-FAHL
lobster	*ıstakoz*
	uhss-tah-KOHZ
mackerel	*uskumru*
	oos-KOOM-roo
mussels	*midye*
	MEED-yeh
plaice	*pisi*
	PEE-see
red coralfish	*mercan*
	mehr-JAHN
red mullet	*barbunya*
	bahr-BOON-yah
roe, red caviar	*tarama*
	tah-rah-MAH
sardine (fresh)	*sardalya*
	sahr-DAHL-yah
sea bass	*levrek*
	lehv-REHK
shrimp	*karides*
	kah-REE-dess

sole	*dil balığı*
	DEEL bah-luh-uh
swordfish	*kılıç balığı*
	kuh-LUHCH bah-luh-uh
trout	*alabalık*
	AH-lah-bah-luhk
tunny, bonito	*palamut*
	PAH-lah-moot
turbot	*kalkan*
	kahl-KAHN

Meats & Kebaps

Most of us think of *kebap* as shish kebab, but in fact *kebap* can refer to anything roasted. Nevertheless, it's usually meat – generally lamb or mutton. Preparation, spices and extras (onions, peppers, *pide*) make for the differences among *kebaps*. The meat may be in chunks, or loaded onto a spit and roasted in front of a vertical grill, then sliced off. Or it may be ground and mixed with spices, then formed into meatballs and charcoal-grilled. Some kebaps may be ordered *yoğurtlu*, with a side-serving of yoghurt.

adana kebap (ah-DAH-nah keh-bahp) – spicy-hot grilled köfte
bonfile (bohn-fee-LEH) – small filet beefsteak
bursa kebap (BOOR-sah keh-bahp) – döner with tomato sauce
    and browned butter
ciğer (jee-EHR) – liver
dana rosto (DAH-nah ROHSS-toh) – roast veal
döner kebap (dur-NEHR keh-bahp) – spit-roasted lamb slices
domuz eti (doh-MOOZ eh-tee) – pork (forbidden to Muslims)
etli pide/etli ekmek (eht-LEE PEE-deh/eht-LEE ehk-MEHK) –
    flat bread topped with ground lamb and spices

güveç (gur-VETCH) – meat-and-vegetable stew in a crock
karışık ızgara (kah-ruh-shuk uhz-gah-rah) – mixed grill (lamb)
köfte (KURF-teh) – grilled lamb meatballs with onion and spices
kuzu (süt) (koo-ZOO (SURT)) – (milk-fed) lamb
musakka (moo-sah-KAH) – aubergine and lamb pie
orman kebap (ohr-MAHN keh-bahp) – roast lamb with onions
piliç (pee-LEECH) – roasting chicken
piliç kızartma (pee-LEECH kuh-ZART-mah) – roast chicken
pirzola (PEER-zoh-lah) – cutlet (usually lamb)
saç kavurma (SAHTCH kah-VOOR-mah) – lamb bits fried on an
  inverted wok
sığır (suh-UHR) – beef
şinitzel (shee-NEET-zehl) – wienerschnitzel
şış kebap (SHEESH keh-bahp) – roast skewered lamb chunks
tandır kebap (tahn-DUHR keh-bahp) – lamb roasted in a crock
  underground
tas kebap (TAHSS keh-bahp) – lamb stew
tavuk (tah-VOOK) – boiling chicken

Salads

Each one of the names over leaf are followed by the word *salata*
or *salatası*. You may be asked if you prefer it *sirkeli*, with vinegar
or *limonlu*, with lemon juice; most salads (except *söğüş*) come
with olive oil. If you don't like hot peppers, say *bibersiz*, though
this often doesn't work.

Many visitors are surprised that Turkish chefs do not make
Greek-style salads of sliced tomatoes and cucumbers with olives,
olive oil, and white cheese. The Turks are catching on, but if your
order for a Greek salad meets with incomprehension, order *çoban
salatası* or *söğüş*, and olives, and white cheese, and make your
own.

çoban (choh-BAHN) – chopped mixed tomato, cucumber, hot
    pepper
karışık (kah-ruh-SHUHK) – same as *çoban salatası*
patlıcan (paht-luh-JAHN) – roast aubergine/eggplant purée
söğüş (sur-URSH) – sliced vegetables, no sauce
turşu (toor-SHOO) – pickled vegetables
yeşil (yeh-SHEEL) – green salad

Vegetables
Often a vegetable (*sebze*) is prepared with meat or stock as a
flavouring, along with tomato sauce, olive oil, and a spice.

beans	*fasulye* fah-SOOL-yeh
green (French) beans	*taze fasulye* tah-ZEH fah-sool-yah
red beans	*barbunye* bahr-BOON-yeh
white beans	*kuru fasulye* koo-ROO fah-sool-yeh
cabbage	*lahana* lah-HAH-nah
carrot	*havuç* hah-VOOCH
cauliflower	*karnabahar* kahr-NAH-bah-hahr
chickpeas/garbanzos	*nohut* noh-HOOT
cucumber	*salatalık* sah-LAH-tah-luhk

green pepper/pimiento (sweet)	*yeşil biber* yeh-SHEEL bee-behr
marrow/squash	*kabak* kah-BAHK
okra	*bamya* BAHM-yah
onion	*soğan* soh-AHN
peas	*bezelye* beh-ZEHL-yeh

potato	*patates*
	pah-TAH-tess
spinach	*ıspınak*
	uhs-spuh-NAHK
tomato	*domates*
	doh-MAH-tess

Stuffed Vegetables

stuffed ... (vegetable)	*... dolma(sı)*
	DOHL-mah(suh)
stuffed squash/marrow	*kabak dolması*
	kah-BAHK dohl-mah-suh
stuffed cabbage	*lahana dolması*
	lah-HAH-nah dohl-mah-suh
stuffed vine leaves	*yaprak dolması*
	yah-PRAHK dohl-mah-suh

Fruit

Turkish fruit (*meyva*; plural *meyve* or *meyvalar*) is wonderful, abundant, but very seasonal. It makes the perfect dessert if Turkish sweets are too syrupy for you.

apple	*elma*
	ehl-MAH
apricot	*kayısı*
	KAH-yuh-suh
banana	*muz*
	MOOZ

cherry	*kiraz*
	kee-RAHZ
fig	*incir*
	een-JEER
grapefruit	*greyfurut*
	GREY-foo-root
grapes	*üzüm*
	ur-ZURM
morello (sour) cherry	*vişne*
	VEESH-neh
orange	*portakkal*
	pohr-tahk-KAHL
peach	*şeftali*
	shef-tah-LEE
pear	*armut*
	ahr-MOOT
strawberries	*çilek*
	chee-LEHK
tangerine/mandarin	*mandalin*
	mahn-dah-LEEN
watermelon	*karpuz*
	kahr-POOZ
yellow melon	*kavun*
	kah-VOON

Sweets/Desserts

Many Turkish baked desserts come swimming in sugar syrup.
They're delicious, but very sweet.

baklava (bahk-lah-VAH) – flaky pastry with honey and nuts
dondurma (dohn-DOOR-mah) – ice cream

ekmek kadayıf (ehk-MEHK kah-dah-yuhf) – crumpet in syrup
fırın sütlaç (fuh-ruhn SURT-latch) – baked rice pudding (cold)
komposto (kohm-POHSS-toh) – stewed fruit
krem karamel (KREHM kah-rah-MEHL) – baked caramel custard
pasta (PAHSS-tah) – pastry (not noodles)
sütlaç (SURT-latch) – rice pudding

Drinks

When speaking of drinks, *içki* usually refers to alcoholic beverages, *meşrubat* to soft drinks. If your waiters say *İçecek?* or *Ne içeceksiniz?*, they're asking what you'd like to drink.

The most popular drink in Turkey is certainly *çay*, tea, served in little tulip-shaped glasses, with sugar. If you want milk, *süt*, in your tea, you'll have to ask for it, causing neighbouring tea-drinkers to puzzle on the exotic preferences of foreigners.

A very popular alternative to regular tea is apple tea, *elma çay*. In summer, try *ayran*, a tart, refreshing beverage made by beating yoghurt and mixing it with spring water and a little salt.

As for Turkish coffee, *türk kahvesi*, order it *sade* bitter, without sugar; *az*, with a little sugar; *orta*, middling sweet; or *çok şekerli*, very sweet.

arrak, anise brandy	*rakı* rah-KUH
coffee	*kahve* kahh-VEH
fruit juice	*meyva suyu* mey-VAH soo-yoo
light/dark beer	*beyaz/siyah bira* bey-AHZ/see-YAHH BEE-rah
milk	*süt* SURT
mineral soda (fizzy)	*soda/maden sodası* SOH-dah, mah-DEHN soh-dah-suh
spring (bottled) water (not fizzy)	*memba suyu* mem-BAH soo-yoo
red/white wine	*kırmızı/beyaz şarap* KUHR-muh-ZUH/bey-AHZ shah-RAHP
yoghurt drink	*ayran* 'eye'-RAHN

Paying the Bill

By law, tax is supposed to be included in the price of every item on the menu, and thus you should not pay an extra charge for tax. You may see *KDV dahildir* (Value-Added Tax Included) on the price list. A service charge may be added, but is usually not. In very cheap restaurants, tips are not really expected but some people leave a few coins or small bills. For meals in a restaurant with white tablecloths and courteous waiters, 8% to 10% is normal. In international-class luxury places, 12% to 15% is expected, and 20% is not sniffed at.

May I have the bill, please?	*Hesap lütfen.*	
	heh-SAHP lurt-fehn	
Is service/tax included?	*Servis/vergi dahil mi?*	
	sehr-VEESS/VEHR-gee dah-HEEL mee	
bill/check	*hesap*	
	heh-SAHP	
service charge	*servis ücreti*	
	sehr-VEES urj-reh-tee	
tax	*vergi*	
	VEHR-gee	
tip	*bahşış*	
	bahh-SHEESH	
error	*yanlış*	
	yahn-LUSH	

Some Useful Words & Phrases

black pepper	*kara/siyah biber*	
	kah-RAH/see-YAHH bee-behr	
bread	*ekmek*	
	ehk-MEK	
butter	*tereyağı*	
	TEH-reh-yah-uh	

cheese	*peynir*
	pey-NEER
family/ladies' dining room	*aile salonu*
	ah-yee-LEH sah-loh-noo
fruit jam	*reçel*
	reh-CHEHL
garlic	*sarmısak*
	SAHR-muh-SAHK
honey	*bal*
	BAHL
ice	*buz*
	BOOZ
lemon	*limon*
	lee-MOHN
macaroni/noodles	*makarna*
	mah-KAHR-nah
mild yellow cheese	*kaşar peynir*
	kah-SHAHR pey-neer
olive oil	*zeytinyağı*
	zey-TEEN-yah-uh
olive(s)	*zeytin*
	zey-TEEN
pizza; flat bread	*pide*
	PEE-deh
sugar; candy/sweets	*şeker*
	sheh-KEHR
vinegar	*sirke*
	SEER-keh
Waiter!	*Garson bey!*
	gahr-SOHN bey

(Waiter) please come.	*Bakar mısınız?* bah-KAHR-muh-suh-nuhz
water	*su* SOO

Cooking Terms

rare	*az pişmuş* AHZ peesh-meesh
well done/very done	*iyi pişmuş* ee-YEE peesh-meesh/ 'CHOKE' peesh-meesh
with (white) cheese	*peynirli* pehy-neer-LEE
with ground lamb	*kıymalı* kuhy-mah-LUH
without meat	*etsiz* eht-SEEZ
yoghurt	*yoğurt* yoh-OORT

Shopping

Many Turkish crafts and trades are named simply by the object dealt with followed by the *-ci*, *-cı*, *-cu*, *-cü* suffix. Thus 'book' is *kitap*, 'bookseller' is *kitapçı* (book-person); shoe is *ayakkabı*, cobbler is *ayakkabıcı* (shoe-person).

Where is …?	*… nerede?*
	NEH-reh-deh
the shopping/market district	*çarşı*
	CHAHR-shuh
the covered bazaar	*kapalı çarşı*
	kah-pah-LUH chahr-shuh
a barber	*bir berber*
	beer behr-BEHR
a bookshop	*bir kitapçı*
	beer kee-TAHP-chuh
a chemist/pharmacy	*bir eczane*
	beer EDJ-zah-NEH
a tailor	*bir terzi*
	beer TEHR-zee
a watch-repair shop	*bir saatçi*
	beer sah-AAHT-chee
Do you have …?	*… var mı?*
	VAHR muh
envelopes	*zarf*
	ZARF

paper	*kağıt* kyaa-UHT
laundry detergent	*deterjan* DEH-tehr-ZHAHN
matches	*kibrit* kee-BREET
I want to buy ...	*... satın almak istiyorum.* sah-TUHN ahl-MAHK eess-tee-yoh-room
aspirin	*aspirina* ahss-pee-REE-nah
bottled spring water	*şişede memba suyu* SHEE-sheh-DEH mem-BAH soo-yoo
a carpet	*halı* hah-LUH
leather clothing	*deri giyim* deh-REE gee-YEEM
old copper (items)	*eski bakır* ehss-KEE bah-KUHR
today's newspaper	*bugünkü gazete* boo-GURN-kurr gah-ZEH-teh
an English-language newspaper/magazine	*igilizce bir gazete/mecmua* een-gee-LEEZ-djeh beer gah-ZEH-teh/MEDJ-moo-ah

Where can I buy ...?	... *nereden satın alabilirim?*
	NEH-reh-den sah-TUHN ah-lah-bee-lee-reem
bus tickets	*otobüs biletleri*
	oh-toh-BURSS bee-leht-leh-ree
film	*filim*
	fee-LEEM

Bargaining

In food markets, prices are regulated and bargaining is usually futile, but for most other items bargaining is necessary. Some shops mark prices and stick to them, but others mark them only in order to 'give you a special discount', so bargaining is in order. Remember, there is never an obligation to buy unless the shopkeeper accepts your price. Don't feel guilty about walking away if you cannot agree upon a price.

How many liras/dollars/pounds ...?	... *kaç lira/dolar/sterlin?*
	KAHTCH lee-RAH/doh-LAHR/stehr-LEEN
is this one	*bunu*
	boo-NOO
is that one	*şunu*
	shoo-NOO
is two kg	*iki kilo*
	ee-KEE kee-LOH
is three metres	*üç metre*
	URCH meh-treh
for all of them	*hepsi*
	HEHP-see

(It's) very expensive.	*Çok pahalı.* 'CHOKE' pah-hah-luh
I'll give you …	*… vereceğim.* VEH-reh-JEH-yeem
$20	*yirmi dolar* yeer-MEE doh-LAHR
40,000 TL	*kırk bin lira* KUHRK been lee-rah
£10	*on sterlin* OHN ster-LEEN
Do you have something cheaper?	*Daha ucuz bir şey var mı?* dah-HAH oo-JOOZ beer shey VAHR muh

Clothes

It's very (too) big/small.	*Çok büyük/küçük.* 'CHOKE' bur-YURK/kur-CHURK
Put (try) it on.	*Giyin.* GEE-yeen
It's too short/long.	*Çok kısa/uzun.* 'CHOKE' kuh-SAH/oo-ZOON
It doesn't fit/match.	*Uymaz.* ooy-MAHZ
Do you have a larger/smaller size?	*Daha büyük/küçük var mı?* dah-HAH bur-YURK/kur-CHURK VAHR muh

I don't like the colour.	*Rengi beğenmiyorum.* REHNG-gee bey-EHN-mee-yoh-room
I don't like (it/them).	*Beğenmiyorum.* bey-EHN-mee-yohr-room

Colours

colour	*renk* RENK
another colour	*başka renk* bahsh-KAH renk
black	*siyah* see-YAHH
blue	*mavi* mah-VEE
brown	*kahverengi* KAHH-veh-rehng-gee
green	*yeşil* yeh-SHEEL
pink	*pembe* pehm-BEH
red	*kırmızı* KUHR-muh-ZUH
white	*beyaz* bey-AHZ
yellow	*sarı* sahr-RUH
dark(er)	*(daha) koyu* (dah-HAH) koy-YOO
light(er)	*(daha) açık* (dah-HAH) ah-CHUK

Toiletries

comb	*tarak*
	tah-RAHK
condom	*prezervatif*
	preh-ZEHR-vah-TEEF
facial tissue/paper handkerchief	*kağıt mendili*
	kyaah-UHT mehn-dee-lee
flea powder	*pirelere karşı pudra*
	PEE-reh-leh-REH kahr-shuh poo-drah
hand cream/lotion	*el kremi/losyonu*
	EHL kreh-mee/lohss-yoh-noo
medicine	*ilaç*
	ee-LAHCH
mirror	*ayna*
	AH-yee-NAH
mosquito repellent	*sivrisineğe karşı ilaç*
	see-VREE-see-neh-YEH kahr-shuh ee-LAHCH
sanitary pad	*hijenik kadın bağı*
	HEE-zheh-NEEK kah-DUHN bah-uh
shampoo	*şampuan*
	SHAM-poo-AHN
shaving cream	*traş kremi*
	TRAHSH kreh-mee
soap	*sabun*
	sah-BOON
sticking plaster/adhesive bandage	*tıbbi filaster*
	tub-BEE fee-LAHSS-tehr

sun cream/oil	*güneş kremi/yağı* gur-NEHSH kreh-mee/yah-uh
tampon	*tampon* tahm-POHN
toilet paper	*tuvalet kağıdı* too-vah-LEHT kyaah-uh-duh
toothbrush	*diş fırçası* DEESH fuhr-chah-suh
toothpaste	*diş macunu* DEESH mah-joo-noo

Stationery

book	*kitap* kee-TAHP
dictionary	*lügat/sözlük* lur-GAHT/surz-LURK
magazine	*mecmua* MEDJ-moo-ah
newspaper	*gazete* GAHZ-teh
notebook	*defter* dehf-TEHR
paper	*kağıt* kyaah-UHT
pen (ballpoint)	*tükenmez* TUR-kehn-MEHZ
pencil	*kurşunkalem* koor-SHOON-kah-lehm
postcard	*kartpostal* KAHRT-pohss-TAHL

Camera

My camera doesn't work.

Foto makinam çalışmıyor.
  foh-TOH mah-KEE-nahm
  chah-LUSH-muh-yohr

It shoots too slow/fast.

Yavaş/çabuk çekiyor.
  yah-VAHSH/chah-BOOK
  cheh-kee-yohr

It needs new batteries.

Yeni piller lazım.
  yeh-NEE peel-LEHR lah-
  zuhm

Some Useful Words

battery

pil
  PEEL

film

filim
  fee-LEEM

flash bulb

filaş
  fee-LAHSH

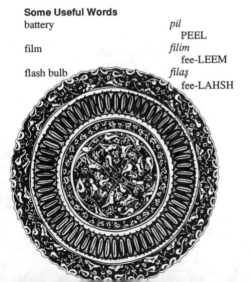

photo	*foto*
	FOH-toh
slide/diapositive	*slayt/diapozitif*
	suh-LAH-eet/DEE-ah-poh
	-zee-TEEF
thirty-six-exposure (film)	*otuz altı poz*
	oh-TOOZ ahl-TUH pohz

Some Useful Words

(hand)bag	*çanta*
	CHAN-tah
brass	*tunç*
	toonch
carpet	*halı*
	hah-LUH
cheap	*ucuz*
	oo-JOOZ
cloth	*kumaş*
	koo-MAHSH
clothing	*elbise/giysi*
	EHL-bee-SEH, GEE-see
copper	*bakır*
	bah-KUHR
expensive	*pahalı*
	pah-hah-LUH
gold	*altın*
	ahl-TUHN
jewellery	*mücevherat*
	mur-JEHV-heh-RAHT
leather	*deri*
	deh-REE

market	*çarşı* chahr-SHUH
meerschaum	*lületaşı* LUR-leh-tah-shuh
pottery (faience)	*çini* CHEE-nee
price	*fiyat* fee-YAHT
shop	*dükkan* durk-KYAHN
silver	*gümüş* gur-MURSH
suede	*süet* sur-WEHT
tax	*vergi* VEHR-gee
this much	*bu kadar* BOO kah-dahr
this one	*bunu* boo-NOO
Which?	*Hangi?* HAHN-gee

Health

Every Turkish city and town has a health facility. In the cities there are hospitals and clinics, both government-run and private; in the towns there are clinics and first-aid stations. All prices are quite low – even at the private hospitals and clinics they are controlled by the government, as are prices for medicines. To find a *hastane* (hospital), look for the standard blue road sign bearing a large 'H' in a white box; for a *klinik* (clinic), or a place providing *ilk yardım* (first aid), look for a blue highway sign bearing a red crescent in a white box. This is the symbol of the Red Crescent Society, the Muslim equivalent of the Red Cross; it's used to indicate any medical facility. You might also see signs pointing the way to the *sağlık memuru* (public health official).

For minor aches and pains, it's customary to go to an *eczane* (chemist or pharmacy) and explain your problem. The *eczacı* (chemist) will sell you a remedy on the spot. Obviously, this is for minor ailments only.

As for doctors, there are general practitioners and specialists in all cities; the bigger the city, the better the health care. Some Turkish ladies observe the custom of having a female friend accompany them if a male doctor makes a physical examination. But as half of all the medical doctors in Turkey are women, choosing your physician by gender is the obvious alternative.

In an Emergency

Many large hospitals have an *acil servis* (emergency service/room) where you can go for quick treatment. If an ambulance is not readily available, a taxi will get you there quickly, hooting the horn all the way (this is understood by other drivers to indicate a medical emergency).

Please call ...	... çağırın.
	chah-UHR-uhn
an ambulance	*cankurtaran/ambulans*
	JAHN-koor-tah-rahn/AHM-bur-LAHNS
a doctor	*doktor/hekim*
	dohk-TOHR/heh-KEEM
the police	*polis*
	poh-LEESS

| It's an emergency. | *Acil vaka var.* |
| | ah-JEEL vah-kah vahr |

Is there ... around here?	*Buralarda ... var mı?*
	BOO-rah-lahr-DAH ... VAHR muh
a hospital	*bir hastane*
	beer HAHSS-tah-NEH
a doctor	*bir doktor/hekim*
	beer dohk-TOHR/heh-KEEM
a chemist/pharmacy	*bir eczane*
	beer EDJ-zah-NEH
a dentist	*bir dişçi/dış hekimi*
	beer DEESH-chee/DEESH heh-kee-mee

How do you feel?	*Nasıl hissediyorsunuz?* NAH-suhl hee-seh-dee-yohr-soo-nooz
I don't feel well.	*Kendimi iyi hissetmiyorum.* KEHN-dee-mee ee-YEE hee- SEHT-mee-yoh-room
I'm ill.	*Hastayım.* hahss-TAH-yuhm
I've caught a cold.	*Üşüdüm.* ur-shur-DURM
I have …	*… var.* vahr
a cold	*nezlem* nehz-LEHM
a fever	*ateşim* ah-tehsh-EEM
diarrhoea	ishalim eess-hah-LEEM
My head's spinning/I'm dizzy.	*Başım dönüyor.* bah-SHUM dur-nur-yohr
I'm going to vomit/be sick.	*Kusacağım geliyor.* KOOSS-ah-JAAH-uhm geh-lee-yohr
I'm/you're pregnant.	*Gebeyim/gebesiniz.* geh-BEH-yeem/geh-BEH-see-neez

Parts of the Body

It hurts here.	*Burası acıyor.* BOO-rah-suh ah-juh-yohr

My ... hurts.   *... ağrıyor.*
aah-ruh-yohr

   arm   *kolum*
koh-LOOM

   back   *sırtım*
suhr-TUHM

   bone   *kemiğim*
keh-mee-YEEM

   breast   *memem*
meh-MEHM

   chest   *göğüsüm*
gur-urss-UHRM

   ear   *kulağım*
koo-laah-UHM

   eye   *gözüm*
gur-ZURM

   finger   *parmağım*
pahr-maah-UHM

   foot   *ayağım*
ah-yaah-UHM

   hand   *elim*
eh-LEEM

head	*başım*
	bah-SHUHM
heart	*kalbim*
	kaal-BEEM
knee(cap)	*diz (kapağı)*
	DEEZ (kah-pah-uh)
leg	*bacağm*
	bah-jaah-UHM
neck	*boynum*
	boy-NOOM
nose	*burnum*
	boor-NOOM
skin	*cildim*
	jeel-DEEM
stomach	*karnım*
	kahr-NUHM
throat	*boğazım*
	BOH-aah-ZUHM
tooth	*dişim*
	dee-SHEEM

Medication

Most modern medicines are available in Turkey, made locally under license. Often the brand name is the same as in English or similar. The generic names of drugs are often similar as well – try the English word, and if that doesn't work, give it a French pronunciation. Modern medical terms often come into Turkish via French, as in *antibiotik* and *antijen*, or my favourite, *tantürdiyot* 'tincture d'iode' – tincture of iodine!

How many times a day?	*Günde kaç defa?* GURN-deh KATCH deh-fah
Four times a day.	*Günde dört defa.* GURN-deh DURT deh-fah
Once every six hours.	*Her altı saatte bir defa.* hehr ahl-TUH saa-AHT-TEH BEER deh-fah
Are there side effects?	*Yan etkisi var mı?* YAHN eht-kee-see VAHR muh
I'm allergic to penicillin.	*Penisiline karşı alerjim var.* nee-see-lee-NEH kahr-shuh ah-lehr-ZHEEM vahr

Some Useful Words & Phrases

Don't do it!	*Yapmayın!* YAHP-mah-yuhn
AIDS (Acquired Immune Deficiency Syndrome)	*aids* eydz
appendicitis	*apandisit* ah-PAHN-dee-SEET
bleeding	*kanama* kah-nah-MAH
blood pressure (high/low)	*(yüksek/düşük) tansiyon* yurk-SEK/dur-SHURK TAHN-see-YOHN
cholera	*kolera* KOH-leh-rah
constipation	*kabız* kaa-BUHZ

cough	*öksürük*
	URK-surr-URK
cramp	*kasınç/kramp*
	kah-SUNCH/KRAHMP
diabetes	*şeker hastalığı*
	sheh-KEHR hahss-tah-luh-uh
disease/illness	*hastalık*
	HAHSS-tah-LUHK
hepatitis/jaundice	*sarılık*
	SAH-ruh-LUHK
influenza	*grip*
	GREEP
injection ('needle')	*iğne*
	EE-neh
malaria	*sıtma*
	SUHT-mah
nausea	*mide bulantısı*
	MEE-deh boo-lahn-tuh-suh
operation	*ameliyat*
	ah-MEH-lee-YAHT
pill	*hap*
	HAHP
pneumonia	*zatürree*
	ZAH-tur-REE
rabies	*kuduz hastalığı*
	koo-DOOZ hahss-tah-luh-uh
serious disease	*ciddi hastalık*
	jeed-DEE hahss-tah-luhk

sprain	*burkulma* boor-kool-MAH
venereal disease	*zührevi hastalık* zurhh-reh-VEE hahss-tah-luhk
vomit/to vomit	*kusma/kusmak* KOOSS-mah, kooss-MAHK
x-ray	*röntgen* RURNT-gehn

Times & Dates

Time

Turks use both the 12-hour and 24-hour clocks, as in Europe. The 24-hour clock is the more formal system used in print and conversation. The 12-hour system is more casual.

Telling the Time

Time is easy if it's 'on the hour' or 'half past'. Just say *saat* (hour) and the number, or in the case of half past, the number plus *buçuk*. Other times are more complicated. For present time, use the hour, the minutes, and ... *geçiyor* (... is passing) or ... *kalıyor* (... is remaining). For a past or future time, use *geçe* and *kala* instead. Either *on beş* (fifteen) or *çeyrek* (quarter) can be used to say 'fifteen past' or 'quarter to', etc.

What time is it? ('how many hours?')	*Saat kaç?* sah-AHT kahtch
It's 8 o'clock.	*Saat sekiz.* sah-AHT seh-KEEZ
It's half past three. ('hour three-one half')	*Saat üç buçuk.* sah-AHT URCH-boo-chook
It's 14.15.	*Saat on dördü on beş geçiyor.* sah-AHT OHN dur-du ohn-BESH geh-chee-yohr

It's twenty to twelve.	*Saat on ikiye yirmi kalıyor.* sah-AHT OHN ee-kee-YEH yeer-MEE kah-luh- yohr
The bus leaves at 6.10.	*Otobüs saat altıyı on geçe kalkar.* oh-toh BURSS sah-AHT AHL-tuh-yuh OHN geh-cheh kahl-kahr
The train should arrive at 18 minutes to seven.	*Tren saat yediye on sekiz kala gelmeli.* trehn sah-AHT yeh-dee-YEH OHN seh-KEEZ kah-lah gehl-meh-lee

When?

When?	*Ne zaman?* NEH zah-mahn
In 20 minutes.	*Yirmi dakikada.* yeer-MEE dahk-kah-dah
Nine hours from now. ('from nine hours-after') Nine hours afterwards.	*Dokuz saat sonra.* doh-KOOZ sah-AHT sohn-rah *Dokuz saattan sonra.* doh-KOOZ sah-AHT sohn-rah
Five hours and 35 minutes before.	*Beş saat otuz beş dakika evvel.* BESH sah-aht oh-tooz BESH dah-kee-kah evv-VEHL
How many hours does it take?	*Kaç saat sürer?* KAHCH sah-aht sur-REHR
It takes … hours.	*… saat sürer.* sah-AHT sewr-rehr

It takes ... minutes.	*... dakika/dakka sürer.*
	dah-kee-KAH/dahk-KAH
	sur-rehr

Some Useful Words & Phrases

When?/What time?	*Ne zaman?*
	NEH zah-mahn
morning	*sabah*
	sah-BAHH
afternoon	*öğleden sonra*
	urr-leh-DEHN sohn-rah
evening	*akşam*
	ahk-SHAHM
night	*gece*
	GEH-jeh
at night	*geceleyin*
	GEH-jeh-LEY-een
in the afternoon	*öğleden sonra*
	urr-leh-DEHN sohn-rah
in the evening	*akşamda*
	ahk-shahm-DAH

in the morning	*sabahleyin*
	sah-BAHH-ley-een
today	*bugün*
	BOO-gurn
tomorrow	*yarın*
	YAHR-uhn
yesterday	*dün*
	DURN
this week/month	*bu hafta/ay*
	BOO hahf-tah/'eye'
next week/month	*gelecek hafta/ay*
	geh-leh-JEHK hahf-tah/ 'eye'
last week/month	*geçen hafta/ay*
	geh-CHEN hahf-tah/'eye'
now	*şimdi*
	SHEEM-dee
soon/right away	*yakında/hemen*
	YAH-kuhn-DAH/HEH-men
early/late	*erken/geç*
	ehr-KEHN/GETCH
fast/slow	*çabuk/yavaş*
	chah-BOOK/yah-VAHSH
every hour/day/month, etc	*her saat/gün/ay*
	HEHR sah-aht/gurn/'eye'
hour	*saat*
	sah-AHT
minute	*dakika/dakka*
	DAH-kee-KAH/ dahk-KAH
second (time)	*saniye*
	SAH-nee-yeh

sometimes	*bazen* BAH-zehn

Dates

Note that the Muslim religious 'day', like the Jewish one, begins at sundown, not at midnight, so a festival to be held on the 25th of the month will run from sundown on the 24th to sundown on the 25th. Also, as with Jewish holidays, many shops and offices in Turkey close for the afternoon before the holiday, called the 'eve' (*arife* – AH-ree-FEH).

What Day Is It?

What day is today?	*Bugün hangi gün?* BOO-gurn HAHN-gee gurn
Today is Tuesday. ('Tuesday-day')	*Bugün salı günü.* BOO gurn sah-LUH gur-nur
What's today's date? ('today the-month's how-many')	*Bugün ayın kaçı?* BOO-gurn AH-yuhn kah-CHUH
Today is the eighteenth. ('today the-month's-eighteenth')	*Bugün ayın onsekizinci.* BOO-gurn AH-yuhn ohn-seh-KEE-zeen-JEE
Today is 23 July. ('today 23 July')	*Bugün yirmiüç temmuz.* BOO-gurn yeer-mee-URCH tehm-MOOZ

Days of the Week

day	*gün* GURN

week	*hafta*
	hahf-TAH
Sunday	*pazar*
	pah-ZAHR
Monday	*pazartesi*
	pah-ZAHR-teh-see
Tuesday	*salı*
	sah-LUH
Wednesday	*çarşamba*
	char-shahm-BAH
Thursday	*perşembe*
	pehr-shehm-BEH
Friday	*cuma*
	joo-MAH
Saturday	*cumartesi*
	joo-MAHR-teh-see

Months of the Year

month	*ay*
	'eye'
year	*sene/ yıl*
	SEH-neh/ YUHL
January	*ocak*
	oh-JAHK
February	*şubat*
	shoo-BAHT
March	*mart*
	MAHRT
April	*nisan*
	nee-SAHN

May	*mayıs*
	mah-YUSS
June	*haziran*
	HAH-zee-RAHN
July	*temmuz*
	tehm-MOOZ
August	*ağustos*
	AH-oo-STOHSS
September	*eylül*
	ey-LURL
October	*ekim*
	eh-KEEM
November	*kasım*
	kah-SUHM
December	*aralık*
	ah-rah-LUHK

Some Useful Words & Phrases

When will you come (back)?	*Ne zaman geleceksiniz?*
	NEH zah-mahn geh-leh-jehk-see-neez
When will it be ready?	*Ne zaman hazır olacak?*
	NEH zah-mahn hah-ZUHR oh-lah-jahk
I will stay for four days/weeks.	*Ben dört gün/hafta kalacağım.*
	behn DURT gurn/hahf-TAH kah-lah-jah-uhm

Numbers

Once you learn the numbers from one to 10, plus 'hundred', 'thousand', and 'half', you can recognise or say any Turkish number, as all numbers are constructed simply of these building blocks.

Cardinal Numbers

1	*bir*
	BEER
2	*iki*
	ee-KEE
3	*üç*
	URCH
4	*dört*
	DURT
5	*beş*
	BESH
6	*altı*
	ahl-TUH
7	*yedi*
	yeh-DEE
8	*sekiz*
	seh-KEEZ
9	*dokuz*
	doh-KOOZ
10	*on*
	OHN

11	*on bir*	ohn BEER
12	*on iki*	ohn ee-KEE
13	*on üç*	ohn URCH
20	*yirmi*	yeer-MEE
30	*otuz*	oh-TOOZ
40	*kırk*	KUHRK
50	*elli*	ehl-LEE
60	*altmış*	ahlt-MUSH
70	*yetmiş*	yeht-MEESH
80	*seksen*	sek-SEHN
90	*doksan*	dohk-SAHN
100	*yüz*	YURZ
101	*yüz bir*	yurz BEER
200	*iki yüz*	ee-KEE yurz
1000	*bin*	BEEN

2000	*iki bin*
	ee-KEE been
10,000	*on bin*
	OHN been
1000,000	*milyon*
	meel-YOHN

Some Cardinal Numbers

Turks tend to run the number words together into one huge word. In these examples the words are separated for easy recognition:

24	*yirmi dört*
	YEER-mee DURT
159	*yüz elli dokuz*
	YURZ ehl-LEE doh-KOOZ
10,501	*on bin beş yüz bir*
	OHN been BESH yurz BEER
346,217	*üç yüz kırk altı bin iki yüz on yedi*
	URCH yurz KURK ahl-TUH been ee-KEE yurz OHN yeh-DEE

Fractions

¼	*çeyrek*
	chey-REK
½ (used alone, eg 'I want half')	*yarım*
	YAH-ruhm
½ (with a number, eg '1½')	*buçuk*
	boo-CHOOK

Ordinal Numbers

Ordinal numbers consist of the number plus the suffix *-inci, -ıncı, -uncu,* or *-üncü,* depending upon 'vowel harmony'. In writing an ordinal number, a full stop (.) abbreviates the suffix. Thus *birinci* and 1. mean the same thing and are pronounced the same way, 'beer-EEN-jee'.

first	*birinci*
	beer-EEN-jee
second	*ikinci*
	ee-KEEN-jee
sixth	*altıncı*
	ahl-TUHN-juh
thirteenth	*onüçüncü*
	ohn-ur-CHURN-jur
fifty-eighth	*ellisekizinci*
	ehi-LEE-seh-keez-EEN-jee
hundredth	*yüzüncü*
	yurz-URN-jur
hundred and seventy-seventh	*yüzyetmişyedinci*
	YURZ yeht-MEESH-yeh-DEEN-jee

Vocabulary

A

accident	*kaza* kah-ZAH
ache	*ağrı* aah-RUH
aeroplane	*uçak* oo-CHAHK
after	*sonra* SOHN-rah
afternoon	*öğleden sonra* UR-leh-DEHN sohn-rah
again/repeat	*yine/tekrar* YEE-neh/tek-RAHR
agriculture	*tarım/ziraat* tah-RUHM/zee-ra-AHT
air conditioning	*klima* KLEE-mah
air mail	*uçakla/uçak ile* oo-CHAHK-lah/oo-CHAHK-ee-leh
alight (disembark)	*inmek* een-MEHK
all	*hepsi/bütün* HEP-see/bur-TURN
alone	*yalnız* yahl-NUHZ

always	*her zaman* HEHR-zah-mahn
America	*Amerika* ah-MEH-ree-kah
and	*ve* VEH
animal	*hayvan* 'hi'-VAHN
another one (one more)	*bir daha* BEER dah-HAH
antique	*antika* ahn-TEE-kah
art	*sanat* sah-NAHT
artist	*sanatçı* sah-naht-CHUH

ashtray	*kül tablası* KURL tah-blah-suh
Asia	*Asya* AHSS-yah
ask (verb)	*sormak* sohr-MAHK
At what time?	*Saat kaçta?* saa-AAHT KAHCH-tah
Australia(n)	*Avustralya(lı)* AH-voo-STRAHL-yah(-luh)

B

bad	*fenah* feh-NAH
bag	*çanta* CHAHN-tah
baggage	*bagaj* bah-GAZH
bank	*banka* BAHN-kah
barber	*berber* behr-BEHR
basket	*sepet* seh-PEHT
bath	*banyo* BAHN-yoh
bathe	*banyo yapmak* BAHN-yoh yahp-mak
bathe (swim) (verb)	*yüzmek* yurz-MEHK

bathroom	*banyo* BAHN-yoh
battery (dry)	*pil* PEEL
battery (car)	*akü/akümülatör* AH-kur/AH-kurm-yur-lah- TUER
be (verb)	*olmak* ohl-MAHK
beach	*plaj* PLAZH
beans	*fasulye* fah-SOOL-yeh
beautiful	*güzel* gur-ZEHL
because	*çünkü* CHURN-kur
bed	*yatak* yah-TAHK
beef	*sığır* suh-UHR
beer	*bira* BEE-rah
before	*evvel/önce* ehv-VEHL/URN-jeh
better	*daha iyi* dah-HAH ee-yee
between	*arasında* AH-rah-suhn-DAH
bicycle	*bisiklet* bee-seke-LEHT

big	*büyük*
	bur-YURK
blanket	*battaniye*
	bah-TAH-nee-yeh
bleed	*kanama*
	KAH-nah-MAH
blood	*kan*
	KAHN
board (embark)	*binmek*
	been-MEHK
boat	*kayık/sandal*
	kah-YUHK/sahn-DAHL
(motor)boat	*motor*
	moh-TOHR
boil	*kaynamak*
	KAH-yee-nah-MAHK
boiled	*kaynamış*
	KAH-yee-nah-MUHSH
book	*kitap*
	kee-TAHP
border (frontier)	*sınır*
	suh-NUHR
both	*ikisi*
	EE-kee-see
bottle	*şişe*
	SHEE-sheh
bowl	*tas*
	TAHSS
boy	*oğlan*
	oh-LAHN

bread	*ekmek* ehk-MEHK
breakfast	*kahvaltı* KAHH-vahl-TUH
bridge (noun)	*köprü* kur-PRUR
bring (verb)	*getirmek* GEH-teer-MEHK
bring ...!	*... getirin!* geh-TEE-reen
broken	*bozuk/kırık* boh-ZOOK/kuh-RUHK
building	*bina* BEE-nah
burn (noun)	*yanık* yah-NUHK
burn (verb)	*yanmak* yahn-MAHK
bus	*otobüs* oh-toh-BURSS
but	*ama/fakat* AH-mah/FAH-kaht
butter	*tereyağı* TEH-reh-yah-uh
buy (verb)	*satın almak* sah-TUHN ahl-mahk

C

calm	*sakin* saah-KEEN
Canada	*Kanada* KAH-nah-dah

candle	*mum*
	MOOM
car/wagon	*araba*
	AH-rah-bah
Careful!	*Dikkat!*
	deek-KAHT
carpet	*halı*
	hah-LUH
central heating	*kalorifer*
	kah-LOH-ree-FEHR
chair	*sandalye*
	sahn-DAHL-yeh
change (money)	*kambiyo*
	KAHM-bee-yoh
cheap	*ucuz*
	oo-JOOZ
chemist (pharmacy)	*eczane*
	EDJ-zah-NEH
chicken	*tavuk/piliç*
	tah-VOOK/pee-LEECH
child	*çocuk*
	choh-JOOK
chocolate	*çikolata*
	CHEE-koh-LAH-tah
cigarette	*sigara*
	see-GAH-rah

cinema	*sinema* SEE-neh-MAH
clean (adjective)	*temiz* teh-MEEZ
closed	*kapalı* kah-pah-LUH
coffee	*kahve* kahh-VEH
cold (temperature)	*soğuk* soh-OOK
cold (ailment)	*nezle* nehz-LEH
cold water	*soğuk su* soh-OOK soo
colour	*renk* REHNK
Come!	*Gelin(iz)!* GEH-leen(-eez)
comfortable	*rahat* rah-HAHT
commerce	*ticaret* tee-jah-REHT
complaint	*şikayet* SHEE-kyah-YEHT
cook (verb)	*pişirmek* PEE-sheer-MEHK
corner	*köşe* kur-SHEH
cotton	*pamuk* pah-MOOK

country (nation)	*memleket* MEHM-leh-KEHT
crab	*yengeç* yehn-GETCH
crossroads	*kavşak* kahv-SHAHK
cup	*fincan* feen-JAHN

D

damp	*nemli* nehm-LEE
dark (colour)	*koyu* koh-YOO
darkness	*karanlık* kah-rahn-LUHK
date (in history)	*tarih* taah-REEHH
delicious	*nefis* neh-FEESS
dessert/tasty	*tatlı* taht-LUH
diarrhoea	*ishal* eess-HAHL
different	*farklı* fahrk-LUH
difficult	*zor* ZOHR
dinner	*akşam yemeği* ahk-SHAHM yeh-meh-yee

dirty/soiled	*pis/kirli* PEESS/KEER-lee
disembark	*inmek* een-MEHK
dive (verb)	*dalmak* dahl-MAHK
doctor	*doktor/hekim* dohk-TOHR/heh-KEEM
do (verb)	*etmek/yapmak* eht-MEHK/yahp-MAHK
door	*kapı* kah-PUH
dormitory	*yatakhane/yurt* yah-TAHK-hah-neh/YOORT
dozen	*düzine* dur-ZEE-neh
dress (noun)	*elbise* EHL-bee-SEH
drink (alcoholic)	*içki* eech-KEE
drink (verb)	*içmek* eech-MEHK
dry (adjective)	*kuru* koo-ROO
dry (verb)	*kurutmak* KOO-root-MAHK
dry cleaning	*kuru temizleme* koo-ROO teh-meez-leh-meh

E

early	*erken* ehr-KEHN
east	*doğu* doh-OO
easy	*kolay* koh-LAH-yee
eat	*yemek* yeh-MEHK
egg	*yumurta* yoo-moor-TAH
electricity	*elektrik* eh-lehk-TREEK
embassy	*büyükelçilik* bur-YURK-ehl-chee-leek
empty	*boş* BOHSH
engineer	*mühendis* MUR-hehn-DEESS
England	*ingiltere* EEN-geel-TEH-reh
enough	*yeter* yeh-TEHR
envelope	*zarf* ZAHRF
Europe	*Avrupa* ahv-ROO-pah
evening	*akşam* ahk-SHAHM
expensive	*pahalı* PAH-hah-LUH

F

face (noun)	*yüz* YURZ
faint (verb)	*bayılmak* BAH-yuhl-MAHK
fan	*vantilatör* VAHN-tee-lah-TEUR
far	*uzak* oo-ZAHK
faucet	*musluk* mooss-LOOK
fear (noun/verb)	*korku/korkmak* kohr-KOO/kohrk-MAHK
fever ('fire')	*ateş* ah-TESH

film	*filim* fee-LEEM
find (verb)	*bulmak* bool-MAHK
fish (noun)	*balık* bah-LUHK
flashlight	*el feneri* EHL feh-neh-ree
flight (aeroplane)	*uçuş* oo-CHOOSH
'flu	*grip* GREEP
food	*yemek* yeh-MEHK
for ...	*... için* ee-CHEEN
foreigner	*yabancı* YAH-bahn-JUH
forest	*orman* ohr-MAHN
fork (utensil)	*çatal* chah-TAHL
fountain	*çeşme* CHESH-meh
fresh	*taze* tah-ZEH
friend	*arkadaş* AHR-kah-DAHSH
full	*dolu* doh-LOO

G

garden	*bahçe*
	BAHH-cheh
genuine	*gerçek*
	gehr-CHEK
German	*Alman*
	ahl-MAHN
girl/daughter	*kız*
	KUHZ
glass (window)	*cam*
	JAHM
glass (drinking)	*bardak*
	bahr-DAHK
glasses (eye)	*gözlük*
	gurz-LURK
go	*gitmek*
	geet-MEHK
Go!	*Gidin!*
	GEE-deen
good	*iyi*
	ee-YEE
goodbye (departing)	*allaha ısmarladık*
	ah-LAHSS-mahr-lah-duhk
goodbye (remaining)	*güle güle*
	gur-LEH gur-LEH
grill (verb)	*ızgara*
	uhz-GAH-rah
guest	*misafir*
	MEESS-ah-FEER
guide (noun)	*mihmandar*
	MEEHH-mahn-DAHR

H

hand-made	*el işi* EHL ee-shee
happy	*mutlu* moot-LOO
harbour	*liman* lee-MAHN
hat/cap	*şapka* shahp-KAH
head (noun)	*baş* BAHSH
heat (noun)	*sıcaklık* suh-JAHK-luhk
heating (noun)	*ısıtma* uh-suht-MAH
heating (central)	*kalorifer* kah-LOH-ree-FEHR
heavy	*ağır* aah-UHR
help/assistance	*yardım* yahr-DUHM
Help!	*İmdat!* eem-DAHT
help yourself	*buyurun(uz)* BOOY-roon-(ooz)
here	*burada* BOO-rah-dah
hill	*tepe* TEH-peh
hire/rent (verb)	*kiralamak* KEE-rah-lah-MAHK

holiday/vacation	*tatil*
	taah-TEEL
honest	*dürüst*
	dur-RURST
hospital	*hastane*
	HAHSS-tah-NEH
hot	*sıcak*
	suh-JAHK
hot water	*sıcak su*
	suh-JAHK soo
hot/cold	*sıcak/soğuk*
	suh-JAHK/soh-OOK
hotel	*otel*
	oh-TEHL
hour	*saat*
	sah-AHT

How?	*Nasıl?*
	NAH-suhl
How many?	*Kaç?*
	KAHCH
How much?	*Ne kadar?*
	NEH kah-dahr
(my) husband	*koca(m)*
	KOH-jah(m)

I

ice cream	*dondurma*
	DOHN-door-MAH
identification (document)	*kimlik*
	KEEM-leek
immediately	*hemen*
	HEH-mehn
India	*Hindistan*
	HEEN-dee-stahn
indigestion	*hazımsızlık*
	HAH-zuhm-SUHZ-luhk
infection	*bulaşma*
	boo-lahsh-MAH
injection ('needle')	*iğne*
	EE-neh
insect	*böcek*
	bur-JEHK
inside	*içerde*
	EE-chehr-DEH
Ireland	*İrlonda*
	eer-LOHN-dah

island
ada
AH-dah

J

jewellery
mücevherat
mur-JEHV-heh-RAHT

job/work
iş
EESH

journalist
gazeteci
GAHZ-teh-jee

… juice ('… water')
… suyu
soo-yoo

K

key
anahtar
ah-nah-TAHR

knife
bıçak
buh-CHAHK

know (knowledge) (verb)
bilmek
beel-MEHK

know (acquaintance) (verb)
tanımak
TAH-nuh-MAHK

L

lake
göl
GURL

lamp
lamba
LAHM-bah

language	*dil//lisan* DEEL/lee-SAHN
late	*geç* GETCH
later ('after')	*sonra* SOHN-rah
laundry (dirty clothes)	*çamaşır* chah-mah-SHUHR
lawyer	*avukat* AH-voo-KAHT
learn	*öğrenmek* UHR-rehn-MEHK
left (hand, side)	*sol* SOHL
letter (mail)	*mektup* mehk-TOOP
light (weight)	*hafif* hah-FEEF
light bulb	*ampül* ahm-PURL
light(s)	*ışık(lar)* uh-SHUHK(-LAHR)
like (verb)	*beğenmek* bey-yehn-MEHK
like (similar)	*benzer* behn-ZEHR
Listen!	*Dinleyin!* deen-LEH-yeen
little (amount)	*az* AHZ

look (verb)	*bakmak* bahk-MAHK
love (affection)	*sevgi* sehv-GEE
love (romantic)	*aşk* ASHK
lover	*aşık/sevgili* aah-SHUHK/SEHV-gee-LEE
luggage	*bagaj* bah-GAZH
lunch	*öğle yemeği* ur-LEH yeh-meh-yee

M

man/person	*adam/insan* ah-DAHm/een-SAHN
map	*harita* HAH-ree-TAH
married	*evli* ehv-LEE
Are you married?	*Evli misiniz?* ehv-LEE-mee-see-neez
I'm married.	*Evliyim.* ehv-LEE-yeem
marry	*evlenmek* ehv-lehn-MEHK
matches	*kibrit* kee-BREET
maximum (adjective)	*en çok/azami* EHN 'choke'/ah-zah-MEE

medicine	*ilaç* ee-LAHCH
milk	*süt* SURT
minimum (adjective)	*en az/asgari* EHN ahz/ahss-gah-REE
minute (time)	*dakika* DAH-kee-KAH
mirror	*ayna* AH-yee-NAH
mistake	*yanlış* yahn-LUSH
money	*para* PAH-rah
month	*ay* 'eye'
more	*daha* dah-HAH
morning	*sabah* sah-BAHH
museum	*müze* MUR-zeh
music	*müzik* mur-ZEEK
mutton ('sheep meat')	*koyun eti* koh-YOON eh-tee

N

name (noun)	*ad* AHD

near	*yakın*
	yah-KUHN
needle	*iğne*
	EE-neh
new	*yeni*
	yeh-NEE
New Zealand	*Yeni Zelanda*
	yeh-NEE zeh-LAHN-dah
newspaper	*gazete*
	gah-ZEH-teh/GAHZ-teh
night	*gece*
	GEH-jeh
no	*hayır*
	HAH-yuhr
noise	*gürültü*
	GUER-euhl-TEU
noisy	*gürültülü*
	geur-EUHL-tur-LUR
none	*yok*
	YOHK
north	*kuzey*
	koo-ZEY
not ...	*... değil*
	dey-YEEL
now	*şimdi*
	SHEEM-dee
number	*numara*
	NOO-mah-rah
number (count) (noun)	*sayı*
	sah-YUH

O

old (thing) (adjective)	*eski* ess-KEE
old/aged (person)	*yaşlı* yahsh-LUH
only	*yalnız* yahl-NUHZ
open (adjective)	*açık* ah-CHUHK
open (verb)	*açmak* ahch-MAHK
or	*veya* vey-YAH
order (food) (verb)	*ısmarlamak* uhss-MAHR-lah-MAHK
orange	*portakkal* POHR-tahk-KAHL

(the) other	*öbür*
	eu-BEUR
(an)other	*başka*
	bahsh-KAH
outside	*dışarda*
	DUH-shahr-DAH

P

pain	*acı*
	ah-JUH
pair (noun)	*çift*
	CHEEFT
painting (noun)	*resim*
	reh-SEEM
parcel	*koli*
	KOH-lee
pardon me	*affedersiniz*
	AHF-feh-DEHR-see-neez
pardon	*pardon*
	pahr-DOHN
park (noun)	*park*
	PARK
passport	*pasaport*
	PAH-sah-PORT
pepper	*biber*
	bee-BEHR
pharmacy/chemist	*eczane*
	EDJ-zah-NEH
plate	*tabak*
	tah-BAHK

platform (train/bus)	*peron* peh-ROHN
please	*lütfen* LURT-fehn
poison(ous)	*zehir(li)* zehh-HEER(-LEE)
police	*polis* poh-LEESS
police officer	*polis memuru* poh-LEESS meh-moo-roo
pork ('pig meat')	*domuz eti* doh-MOOZ eh-tee
post (verb)	*postalamak* POHSS-tah-lah-MAHK
post office	*postane* POHSS-tah-neh
postcard	*kartpostal* KAHRT-pohss-TAHL
prescription	*reçete* REH-cheh-TEH
prostitute	*orospu* OH-rohss-poo
province	*il/vilayet* EEL/vee-lah-YEHT

Q

quality	*nitelik/kalite* NEE-teh-LEEK/KAH-lee-TEH
question (noun)	*soru* soh-ROO

quick	*çabuk*
	chah-BOOK
quiet (adjective)	*sakin*
	saah-KEEN

R

railway	*demiryolu*
	deh-MEER-yoh-loo
railways	*demiryolları*
	deh-MER-yoh-lah-ruh
rain (noun)	*yağmur*
	yaah-MOOR
razor	*ustura*
	ooss-too-RAH
razor (electric)	*traş makinası*
	TRAHSH mah-kee-nah-suh
receipt	*makbuz*
	mahk-BOOZ
rent (verb)	*kiralamak*
	KEE-rah-lah-MAHK
rent (noun)	*kira parası*
	kee-RAH pah-rah-suh
repair (verb)	*tamir etmek*
	tah-MEER eht-mehk
repairs	*tamirat*
	TAH-mee-RAHT
repeat (verb)	*tekrarlamak*
	tehk-RAHR-lah-MAHK
Repeat!	*Tekrarlayım!*
	TEHK-rahr-LAH-yuhn

reservation	*rezervasyon* REH-zehr-vahss-YOHN
rest (verb)	*dinlenmek* DEEN-lehn-MEHK
restaurant	*lokanta* loh-KAHN-tah
return (come back)	*dönmek* durn-MEHK
rice (uncooked)	*pirinç* pee-REENCH
rice (cooked)	*pilav* pee-LAHV
right (side)	*sağ* SAAH
river	*nehir/ırmak* neh-HEER/uhr-MAHK
road	*yol* YOHL
roof	*çatı* chah-TUH
room	*oda* OH-dah

S

salt	*tuz* TOOZ
sandal	*sandalet* SAHN-dah-LEHT
scenery	*manzara* MAHN-zah-RAH

Scotland	*İskoçya*
	eess-'COACH'-yah
sea	*deniz*
	deh-NEEZ
seat (bus, train) ('place')	*yer*
	YEHR
seat (safety) belt	*emniyet kemeri*
	EHM-nee-YEHT keh-meh-ree
second (timekeeping)	*saniye*
	SAH-nee-YEH
sell (verb)	*satmak*
	saht-MAHK
send	*göndermek*
	gurn-dehr-MEHK
several	*birkaç*
	beer-KAHCH
sew	*dikmek*
	deek-MEHK
shampoo	*şampuan*
	SHAHM-poo-AHN
shave (verb)	*traş etmek*
	TRAHSH eht-mehk
ship	*gemi*
	geh-MEE
shoe lace	*ayakkabı bağı*
	ay-YAHK-kab-buh baah-uh
shop	*dükkan*
	durk-KYAHN
shopping	*alış-veriş*
	ah-LUSH-veh-REESH

short (length)	*kısa* kuh-SAH
short (height)	*kısa boylu* kuh-SAH boy-loo
shower	*duş* DOOSH
shut (closed)	*kapalı* KAH-pah-LUH
signature	*imza* eem-ZAH
silk	*ipek* ee-PEHK
sleep (verb)	*uyumak* oo-yoo-MAHK
slowly	*yavaş yavaş* yah-VAHSH yah-vahsh
small	*küçük* kur-CHURK
smell (verb)	*koklamak* KOHK-lah-MAHK
smoke (verb) ('drink')	*içmek* eech-MEHK
smoke a cigarette (verb)	*sigara içmek* see-GAH-rah eech-mehk
snow (noun)	*kar* KAHR
snow (verb)	*kar yağmak* KAHR yaah-mahk
soap	*sabun* sah-BOON

south	*güney*
	gur-NEY
South Africa	*Güney Afrika*
	gur-NEY AHF-ree-kah
speak	*söylemek*
	SURY-leh-MEHK
spoon	*kaşık*
	kah-SHUK
stale	*bayat*
	bah-YAHT
stamp (noun)	*pul*
	POOL
stomach	*mide/karın*
	mee-DEH/kah-RUHN
(to) stop	*durmak*
	door-MAHK
Stop!	*Durun!*
	DOO-roon
straight	*doğru*
	doh-ROO
street	*sokak/cadde*
	soh-KAHK/JAHD-deh
student	*öğrenci/talebe*
	uer-rehn-JEE/TAH-leh-BEH
style (fashion)	*moda*
	MOH-dah
sugar/sweets	*şeker*
	sheh-KEHR
sweet (noun or adjective)	*tatlı*
	taht-LUH

swim (verb)	*yüzmek* yurz-MEHK

T

table	*masa* MAH-sah
tablet (medicine)	*hap* HAHP
tailor	*terzi* TEHR-zee
taste/tasty	*tat/tatlı* TAHT/taht-LUH
tax	*vergi* VEHR-gee

tea	*çay*
	CHAH-yee
teacher	*öğretmen/hoca*
	uer-reht-MEHN/HOH-jah
telegram	*telgraf*
	tehl-GHRAF
telephone	*telefon*
	TEH-leh-FOHN
temple	*tapınak/mabed*
	TAH-puh-NAHK/mah-BED
thankyou (informal)	*sağ ol*
	'SOWL' (like 'howl')
thankyou (formal)	*teşekkür ederim*
	tesh-ehk-KEUR eh-deh-reem
thanks	*mersi*
	mehr-SEE
thanks	*teşekkürler*
	tesh-ehk-keur-LEHR
that (one)	*şu(nu)*
	shoo(NOO)
the other (one)	*o(nu)*
	oh(NOO)
theatre	*tiyatro*
	tee-AH-troh
there	*orada*
	OH-rah-dah
this (one)	*bu(nu)*
	boo(NOO)
thread	*iplik*
	EEP-leek

throat	*boğaz* boh-AHZ
ticket(s)	*bilet(ler)* bee-LEHT(LEHR)
toast ('grilled bread')	*kızartmış ekmek* kuh-zahrt-MUHSH ek-mehk
today	*bugün* BOO-gurn
toilet	*tuvalet* too-vah-LEHT
toilet paper	*tuvalet kağıdı* too-vah-LEHT kyah-uh-duh
tomorrow	*yarın* YAHR-uhn
tooth	*diş* DEESH
toothbrush	*diş fırçası* DEESH fuhr-chah-suh
toothpick	*kürdan* kur-DAHN
torch (electric)	*el feneri* EHL feh-neh-ree
tourist	*turist* too-REEST
towel	*havlu* hahv-LOO
toy (noun)	*oyuncak* oy-oon-JAHK
train (noun)	*tren* TREHN

translate	*çevirmek/tercüme etmek* CHEH-veer-MEHK/TEHR-jur-MEH eht-mehk
travel/journey (noun)	*seyahat/yolculuk* sey-yah-HAHT/YOHL-joo-LOOK
travel (verb)	*seyahat etmek* seh-yah-HAHT eht-mehk
Turkish bath	*hamam* hah-MAHM
turn (verb)	*döndürmek* DURN-dur-MEHK

U

ulcer	*ülser* url-SEHR
umbrella	*şemsiye* shem-see-YEH
understand	*anlamak* AHN-lah-MAHK
United Kingdom	*Birleşik Kraliyeti* BEER-leh-SHEEK KRAH-lee-YEH-tee
United States	*Birleşik Amerika* BEER-leh-SHEEK ah-MEH-ree-kah
up(stairs)	*yukarı* YOO-kah-RUH

V

vegetable(s)	*sebze* sehb-ZEH
very	*çok* 'CHOKE'
village	*köy* KEURY
vinegar	*sirke* SEER-keh
vomit (verb)	*kusmak* kooss-MAHK

W

wage (noun)	*maaş* MAAHSH
wait (verb)	*beklemek* BEHK-leh-MEHK
waiter	*garson* gahr-SOHN
want (verb)	*istemek* eess-teh-MEHK
wash (something) (verb)	*yıkamak* YUH-kah-MAHK
wash (oneself) (verb)	*yıkanmak* YUH-kahn-MAHK
watch (noun)	*saat* saah-AHT
wave (noun)	*dalga* dahl-GAH
weather ('air')	*hava* hah-VAH

weight	*ağırlık*
	AAH-uhr-LUHK
week	*hafta*
	hahf-TAH
west	*batı*
	bah-TUH
What does it mean?	*Ne demek?*
	NEH deh-mehk
What's this?	*Bu ne?*
	BOO neh
What?	*Ne?*
	NEH
wheel	*tekerlek*
	TEK-ehr-LEK
When?	*Ne zaman?*
	NEH zah-mahn
Where?	*Nerede?*
	NEH-reh-deh
Which?	*Hangi?*
	HAHN-gee
Which one?	*Hangisi?*
	HAHN-gee-see
Who?	*Kim?*
	KEEM
Why?	*Niçin/Neden?*
	NEE-cheen/NEH-dehn
wife	*karı*
	kah-RUH
(my) wife	*karım*
	kah-RUHM

wine	*şarap*
	shah-RAHP
woman	*kadın/hanım*
	kah-DUHN/hah-NUHM
working hours	*çalışma saatleri*
	chal-ush-MAH sah-aht-leh-ree

X

x-ray	*röntgen*
	RURNT-gehn

Y

year	*yıl/sene*
	YUHL/SEH-neh
yes	*evet*
	eh-VEHT
yesterday	*dün*
	DURN

you're welcome	*bir şey değil*
	beer SHEY dey-YEEL
young/a youth	*genç*
	GENCH

z

zoo	*hayvanat bahçesi*
	'hi'-vah-NAHT bah-cheh-see

Language survival kits

Brazilian phrasebook
A little knowledge of *brasileiro* will give travellers a definite advantage.

Burmese phrasebook
Useful words and phrases, with Burmese script for each, will help you make the most of your stay in Burma.

Hindi/Urdu phrasebook
Hindi and Urdu are closely related languages spoken in north India and Pakistan.

Indonesia phrasebook
A little Indonesian is easy to learn, and as it's almost identical to Malay, this book is doubly useful.

Japanese phrasebook
Includes correct pronunciation and Japanese characters for all words & phrases.

Korean phrasebook
As little English is spoken outside the major cities of Korea, this book is vital for the independent traveller.

China phrasebook
Covers China's official language, Mandarin (*Putonghua*), with *pinyin* spellings & Chinese characters.

Nepal phrasebook
Nepali is spoken in parts of India, Sikkim and Bhutan as well as in Nepal. Includes a chapter on useful phrases when trekking.

Papua New Guinea phrasebook
Pidgin is Papua New Guinea's lingua franca, also spoken with minor variations in Vanuatu and the Solomon islands.

Pilipino phrasebook
Pilipino, also known as Tagalog, is the Philippines' national language and is spoken by almost half the population.

Quechua phrasebook
Quechua (*Runasimi*), the language of the Incas, is still spoken widely in rural Peru and Bolivia.

Sri Lanka phrasebook
This book is for those who want to get off the beaten track and communicate with the local people in Sri Lanka's national language, Sinhala.

Swahili phrasebook
Swahili is widely spoken throughout East Africa – from the coast of Kenya and Tanzania through to Zaire.

Thai phrasebook
This book uses easy-to-follow pronunciation symbols and also includes Thai script.

Tibet phrasebook
Tibetan is spoken in a number of Chinese provinces, and also in Nepal, Sikkim and Ladakh. Tibetan script is included for all phrases.

Travel Survival Kits

Alaska
Argentina
Australia
Baja California
Bali & Lombok
Bangladesh
Bolivia
Brazil
Burma
Canada
Central Africa
Chile & Easter Island
China
Colombia
East Africa
Ecuador & the Galapagos Islands
Egypt & the Sudan
Fiji
Hong Kong, Macau & Canton
India
Indonesia
Israel
Japan
Jordan & Syria
Karakoram Highway
Kashmir, Ladakh & Zanskar
Kathmandu & the Kingdom of Nepal
Korea
Madagascar & Comoros
Malaysia, Singapore & Brunei
Maldives & Is. of the East Indian Ocean
Mauritius, Réunion & Seychelles
Mexico
Micronesia
Morocco, Algeria & Tunisia
New Zealand
Pakistan
Papua New Guinea
Peru
Philippines
Rarotonga & the Cook Islands
Samoa
Solomon Islands
Sri Lanka

Tahiti & French Polynesia
Taiwan
Thailand
Tibet
Tonga
Turkey
West Africa
Yemen

Shoestring Guides

Africa on a shoestring
Eastern Europe on a shoestring
North-East Asia on a shoestring
South America on a shoestring
South-East Asia on a shoestring
West Asia on a shoestring

Trekking & Walking Guides

Bushwalking in Australia
Tramping in New Zealand
Trekking in the Indian Himalaya
Trekking in the Nepal Himalaya
Trekking in Turkey

Phrasebooks

Brazilian phrasebook
Burmese phrasebook
China phrasebook
Hindi/Urdu phrasebook
Indonesia phrasebook
Japanese phrasebook
Korean phrasebook
Nepal phrasebook
Papua New Guinea phrasebook
Pilipino phrasebook
Quechua phrasebook
Sri Lanka phrasebook
Swahili phrasebook
Thai phrasebook
Tibet phrasebook
Turkish phrasebook

And Also

Travel with Children
Traveller's Tales

Lonely Planet travel guides are available round the world.
For a copy of our current booklist or a list of our distributors write to:
Lonely Planet, PO Box 617, Hawthorn, Vic. 3122, Australia
Lonely Planet, Embarcadero West, 112 Linden St, Oakland,
CA 94607, USA